DIVINE HEALING TODAY

DIVINE
HEALING
TODAY

RICHARD
MAYHUE

MOODY PRESS
CHICAGO

All Scripture quotations, unless noted otherwise, are from the *New American Standard Bible*, © 1960, 1962, 1963, 1968, 1971, 1972, 1973, 1975, and 1977 by The Lockman Foundation, and are used by permission.

The use of selected references from various versions of the Bible in this publication does not necessarily imply publisher endorsement of the versions in their entirety.

Material from chapters 2, 3, and 4 and appendixes A, B, C, and D is taken from Richard L. Mayhue, *The Biblical Pattern for Divine Healing* (Winona Lake, Ind.:BMH Books, 1979), and is used by permission.

Library of Congress, Cataloging in Publication Data

Mayhue, Richard L.
Divine healing today.

Bibliography: p. 159
1. Spiritual healing. I. Title.
BT732.5.M4 1983 234'.13 83-9351
ISBN 0-8024-0453-7

R 1 2 3 4 5/GB/87 86 85 84 83
Printed in the United States of America

To Dad, who recently was called home to be with His Lord, and to Mom, whose encouragement and help have been invaluable in my life

Contents

Foreword

When John the Baptist questioned Jesus as to whether He was the Messiah or whether they were to expect another, our Lord replied with an instant personalized series of healings just for John. They were the evidence of His messiahship.

Jesus' power to overrule illness and infirmity of all kinds resulted in His nearly banishing disease altogether from Palestine during the days of His ministry. That power was continued through His apostles.

The prospect of physical healing drew people to Him and His apostles by the thousands. Men and women have always sought relief from the miseries of sickness and disease. And they were not disappointed. They were healed.

This unique and miraculous activity tells us much about the character of God. First, He is compassionate. He knows who suffers and desires to relieve their suffering. Our Lord could have used any display of power to prove His deity, but none would have so indicated His compassion as His healing. The second great truth we see in this ministry of Christ is that God is able to heal any and all disease and sickness.

So, God cares to heal and is able to heal. The remaining

questions are, Does He still heal? And if He does, How and when does He heal?

This excellent book will give you biblical answers to those questions. It should be required reading for every Christian today.

John F. MacArthur, Jr.
Grace Community Church
Sun Valley, Calif.

Introduction

God heals today! To render another verdict is to dismiss the biblical witness. However, that precious truth does raise a number of pressing questions.

How is God healing today?

Is it always God's will to heal?

Will He heal me?

Reuben A. Torrey, former president of Moody Bible Institute, candidly wrote:

I know of no book on the topic of Divine Healing that goes thoroughly into the subject and gives all sides of the truth' in their scriptural proportions. Some see only those passages that emphasize God's ability and readiness to heal our diseases and what He has done to make such healing possible today; others are entirely occupied with those passages that make it clear that God sometimes does not heal or that God has different ways of working in different dispensations. A book is greatly needed that considers with utter impartiality all that God has to say on this subject and that has but one aim, to discover exactly what God teaches on this very important subject, and all He teaches.[1]

Dr. Torrey's balanced counsel is the core around which this study is developed and thus demands that we thoroughly inspect the Scriptures. Our purpose will be to discover all that God has prescribed for physical problems. Only then can we anticipate answers to our questions through the balanced study of God's Word.

Scripture makes both doctrine and experience essential elements in healthy Christianity. An authentic experience of God's truth always issues from the fountainhead of His revealed Word. Few areas of current interest are more confused than divine healing because God's unchanging arrangement of truth and experience is often reversed or ignored.

Misunderstanding the relationship of love to truth also lends itself to frequent error. Love discovers its genesis in truth and is defined as walking "according to His commandments" (2 John 6). Love never determines truth although they are inseparably linked.

Both experience and love are balanced and given expression through God's written testimonies. To say that a loving God would never afflict someone with illness or never allow suffering is to misunderstand both love and the Scriptures (Hebrews 12:1-13). Let us examine the cause of such confusion.

Someone has observed that the Bible is a literary pool in which a child can wade but an elephant can swim. For example, John 3:16 reads rather easily. However, the Ethiopian eunuch needed Philip to interpret the far more difficult Isaiah 53 (see Acts 8:31).

J. Sidlow Baxter makes this classic observation about "elephant-type" texts.

And how endlessly interesting these problem texts make the Bible! Joseph Parker well said: "When the last word has been said about the Bible it will no longer be the Word of God." We never get to the end of the Bible. It is as wise in its reservations as in its revelations. Enough is revealed to make faith intelligent. Enough is reserved to give faith scope for development. Everything needful to salvation and godliness is

---

1. R. A. Torrey, *Divine Healing* (Grand Rapids: Baker, n.d.), p. 5.

written with such clarity that all the simple-hearted may understand; but there are other matters which, with wise divine purpose, are presented less lucidly, or even enigmatically, so as to challenge enquiry—matters fascinating, mysterious, or more intricate, but all yielding rich and sanctifying reward to devout exploration.[2]

The challenge that Baxter highlights is not new. Prophets of old sought to know what person or time the Spirit of Christ within them was indicating. They struggled to reconcile the sufferings of Christ with His glories to follow (1 Peter 1:10-11).

Even Peter had to strain. He noted that some of Paul's letters contained prophetic teachings that were hard to understand (2 Peter 3:15-16).

The theme of divine healing offers the same challenge. Joni Eareckson learned a great lesson while she sifted through her inquiries. Listen to Joni's well-stated discovery.

Often we have questions about issues like this which require more than just simple answers, but we don't have the patience to hear those answers out. Sometimes in the past, my own attitude has been, "Don't give me any detailed theological stuff. Just answer my question." Then, because I refused to take the time or mental energy to hear and consider the answer, I would go away assuming no answer existed.[3]

Answers to tough questions do exist if we patiently and prayerfully seek them. So, with God's Spirit as our "truth guard," let's plunge into the deep end of the pool.

Paul's prayer for us would be "that your love may abound more and more in knowledge and depth of insight, so that you may be able to discern what is best" (Philippians 1:9-10, NIV*).

*New International Version.

2. J. Sidlow Baxter, Studies in Problem Texts (Grand Rapids: Zondervan, 1960), p. 5.

3. Joni Eareckson, A Step Further (Grand Rapids: Zondervan, 1978), p. 108.

Part One

God's Healing Ministry

✦ 1 ✦

The Current Interest
in Divine Healing

Larry and Alice Parker desired God's best for their family of six. Wesley, their oldest son, suffered from diabetes and regularly received insulin injections.

When Daniel Badilla held special services in their Barstow, California, church, the Parkers "walked the aisle" with eleven-year-old Wesley. They were sincerely seeking a miracle of healing.

The preacher pronounced Wesley healed. Larry joyfully entered, "Praise God our son is healed," into Wesley's insulin log. But Wesley's ensuing insulin test indicated differently. By faith, the Parkers claimed the healing and blamed the unexpected insulin results on Satan.

Shortly afterward, Wesley began to suffer the nausea and severe stomach cramps that are predictable indicators of low insulin. They decided to postpone medical attention in favor of seeking God's continued healing power through prayer. Wesley fell into a coma and died three days later.

The account of the tragedy was reported nationally by *Newsweek*.[1]

In Ilorin, Nigeria, a veteran missionary serving under the Sudan Interior Mission was troubled by those claiming to practice divine healing. He was burdened by the excesses and wrote these personal observations: "This is a real problem here. Many are trying to heal. The methods would baffle your mind. I have not seen very much 'biblical healing.'"

A renewed worldwide interest in divine healing is emerging in both secular and Christian circles. Many circumstances have converged to spawn this contemporary reality.

The information explosion in recent decades has recreated the Dark Ages in reverse. During those cruel and gruesome times of intellectual poverty, people were uneducated and did not possess enough knowledge to believe. Today the volume of available knowledge is doubling every decade, and people now do not know *what* to believe. The result is identical—error and ignorance.

A new wave of existential thinking is locking arms with the data deluge. Belief in supposed miracles is a surging reaction to liberal theology with all of its spiritually deadening and unsatisfying effects. This wave has overflowed its biblical boundaries and flooded man's thinking with presumption.

Francis Schaeffer explains such thinking with extraordinary perception.

One can also see a parallel between the new Pentecostals and the liberals. The liberal theologians don't believe in content or in religious truth. They are really existentialists using theological, Christian terminology. Consequently, not believing in truth, they can enter into fellowship with any other experience-oriented group using religious language. A dismissal or lessening of content has occurred in the new Pentecostalism. Instead of accepting a person on the basis of what he believes, which has always been the Christian way, it's, "Do you have these external manifestations?" Questions which have been considered important enough to cause crucial differences, all the way back to the Reformation and before, now are swept under the rug. On this level too, as with the liberals, it is as though people can believe opposite things on important points of doctrine, and both can be right. Or

1. "The Exorcist," *Newsweek*, 10 September 1973, p. 31.

perhaps, it is better to simply say, content does not matter as long as there are the external signs and religious emotion.[2]

"Experiential Christianity" is the in thing today. That mind-set cannot be confined or identified with any one age group or denominational organization. The common denominator that unites divergent groups is experience. They claim that God's reality is inexpressible apart from experience. That thinking has led to multiplied excesses where experience attempts to override divine mandates.

Society is also sicker than ever. A popular periodical reported that the health-care industry has recorded a 50 percent increase in payment for medical services over the last five years. It has exceeded 200 billion dollars in recent years.

The medical profession makes phenomenal advances annually in the raging war against disease. Yet an increasingly sick society, bent on instant cure, turns to whoever offers the quickest path to relief.

Although the charismatic movement has focused new attention on divine healing, no two groups within the movement agree in every detail. Their message usually includes the promise of God's complete and immediate healing if the afflicted responds with full faith. The sick who are without hope from doctors and lie helplessly incapacitated without God's intervention are irresistibly drawn toward such beckoning hope of health.

Faith healing is in vogue. The names of Allen, Bosworth, McCrossan, McPherson, and Price were on the lips of all who sought healing in past decades. So great was their popularity, they became household names.

Today a new generation has been born. Headline healers include Angley, Hagin, Osborn, and Roberts, and their ministries range from hospitals to healing cloths.

Oral Roberts built the "City of Faith"—an impressive medical complex on the Oral Roberts University campus. Medical, dental, and nursing students are trained there. It is only one of many "delivery systems" God uses to heal, according to Roberts. (Roberts uses that phrase on his radio broadcasts.)

2. Francis Schaeffer, *The New Super Spirituality* (Downers Grove, Ill.: Inter-Varsity, 1972), p. 16.

Also operating in the Oklahoma city of Tulsa are faith healers T. L. and Daisy Osborn. In their *Faith Digest* the Osborns advertise:

> Health for your sickness
> Success for your failure
> Love for your loneliness
> Happiness for your distress
> Faith for your fears
> Prosperity for your poverty.

The Osborn Foundation sends a small piece of burlap to the readers of its magazine. It is suggested that the reader write out "the *special miracle* needed from God" and mail it with the piece of cloth to the foundation. Written on the envelope provided is Acts 19:11-12: "And God was performing extraordinary miracles by the hand of Paul, so that handkerchiefs or aprons were even carried from his body to the sick, and the diseases left them and the evil spirits went out." Underneath that the Osborns have written: "After 3 days and 4 nights of fasting and prayer, we'll return this same cloth to you."

They report this personal testimony.

> Recently, a woman with an inoperable and cancerous brain tumor, phoned them [the Osborns]. They were impressed to do like Saint Paul (Acts 19:11-12). They held a piece of burlap cloth in their hands as they prayed for the woman, then they sent it to her as a POINT-OF-CONTACT FOR FAITH. She laid it on her head as she prayed, and was MIRACULOUSLY HEALED. This kind of thing has happened hundreds of times.[3]

Streams of literature complement the faith healing ministry. Such publications are distributed widely and usually contain all sorts of promises and procedures. Here are several.

3. According to a solicitation letter I received by mail from the Osborn Foundation, Box 10, Tulsa, OK 74102.

Dr. Hobart Freeman writes, "When genuine faith is present it alone will be sufficient, for it will take the place of medicine and other aids."[4]

William Caldwell provides an unusual claim.

In order to receive healing, it may not be necessary for you to read this book through to the end. Rather, just take the first nugget of truth that applies to your situation and act upon it. Many people will be healed while reading the first chapter. Therefore, be alert and eager for your opportunity to present itself. Of course, if you do not see yourself being healed in the first pages, read on until you do.[5]

Oral Roberts announces:

I have a feeling that the mass healing of an entire audience is nearer than we think. We have been laying the ground work for it for years. . . . Perhaps some night when all of us are touching someone near us and we offer prayer in concert, we will all understand that our hands are as His hands laid upon the sick and in that moment everyone there will be healed. I am fully expecting this soon.[6]

The church is in a state of confusion over divine healing. Questions like these perplex many. Is it real? If it is not real, how can I explain some of the apparent healings? How does it work? If it does work, why should I ignore or deny a good thing? Why the sudden appearance and increase of healing if it was possible all along? Is it biblical? Why am I sick? Should I quit taking medicine? Why haven't I been healed? Why are some in the healing movement sick? Why do all in the healing movement die?

Maybe you have asked some of those questions yourself. No doubt many of those same inquiries agonized the hearts of the Parkers. Even though they had placed their full faith in God, Wesley died.

4. Hobart Freeman, *Faith* (Claypool, Ind.: Faith Publications, n.d.), p. 11.
5. William Caldwell, *Meet the Healer* (Tulsa: Front Line Evangelism, 1965), p. 5.
6. Oral Roberts, *Seven Divine Aids for Your Health* (Tulsa: Oral Roberts, 1960), p. 35.

A lawyer recently shared with me a letter he received from Larry Parker. Years have passed since Wesley's death. Larry struggled for the truth and found it only as he sought full scriptural counsel. The letter reads:

> I am writing this letter with the hope and prayer that somehow, I can share with you a lesson that I have learned at great expense. It is only by the grace of God, and the never failing, all encompassing, love of Jesus Christ our Lord, that my wife and I have been able to come through this trial.
>
> Although we were greatly confused, we knew that we had to keep our faith in Jesus Christ our Lord. After a few months, my wife was able to accept the fact that Wesley was to stay with Jesus, but for me, it took three years.
>
> We wanted to see our son healed, but went about it the wrong way. It was during our trial for involuntary manslaughter and felony child abuse that my wife felt she could tell me what the Lord had shown her. She told me that our love, because it was lacking, failed Wesley, and that God's word says, "Love never faileth" (1 Corinthians 13:8).
>
> I knew then that we had allowed what we thought was faith to cause us to forget to love. As we prayed for Wesley and saw him in obvious pain, our love for him wanted to give him the insulin that we knew would stop his suffering. However, we felt that would be a lack of faith, and would cost him his healing. We learned that our actions were contrary to what the Scriptures say. God's word says that love is greater than faith (1 Corinthians 13:13).
>
> The trouble lies with the fact that we confuse faith and belief. We think that if we believe hard enough, the healing will take place. We tie healing to some ability on our part to believe enough, i.e., to have enough faith.
>
> To withhold medicine, especially life-giving medicine, is a very presumptuous act on our part that actually hinders the Spirit of God from His work.
>
> My prayer is that you will consider these thoughts at length, for they have come at an incomprehensible price that no one would voluntarily pay.[7]

7. Larry and Alice Parker have recently published their story in *We Let Our Son Die* (Irvine, Calif.: Harvest House, 1980). Larry Parker has given liberty to quote this letter. In doing so, however, the Parkers are not endorsing all of the conclusions reached in this volume.

I am moved by Larry's honesty and the excruciating pain he suffered. The issue is real. The lives of loved ones are involved. God can, has, and does heal; but always for His own purposes, in His own way, and at His appointed time.

So let's consult His record of revealed truth for answers to our questions.

✦ 2 ✦

The Old Testament
Healing Record

Dipping seven times in the river healed a visiting general of incurable leprosy (2 Kings 5:14).

An invading army 185,000 strong died in their sleep on the same night (Isaiah 37:36).

"Boanthropy" suddenly struck a renowned world ruler. Seven years later full health returned, and he resumed his international prominence (Daniel 4:33-34).

What is common to all of those unique events? They all illustrate the Potter's direct involvement in the physical affairs of His human pottery.

God healed Naaman. Sennacherib's Assyrian army expired at God's will. God removed and later reinstated the Babylonian King Nebuchadnezzar.

The Old Testament also records God's explanation.

And the Lord said to him, "Who has made man's mouth? Or who makes him dumb or deaf, or seeing or blind? Is it not I, the Lord?" [Exodus 4:11]

See now that I, I am He, and there is no god besides Me; it is I who put to death and give life. I have wounded, and it is I who heal;

and there is no one who can deliver from My hand. [Deuteronomy 32:39]

Behold, how happy is the man whom God reproves, so do not despise the discipline of the Almighty. For He inflicts pain, and gives relief; He wounds, and His hands also heal. [Job 5:17-18]

The One forming light and creating darkness, causing well-being and creating calamity; I am the Lord who does all these. [Isaiah 45:7]

Who is there who speaks and it comes to pass, unless the Lord has commanded it? Is it not from the mouth of the Most High that both good and ill go forth? [Lamentations 3:37-38]

What a testimony! By His own declaration God is ultimately responsible for health or sickness, life or death. However, meaningful conclusions about God's present involvements are impossible to draw before the biblical record is consulted. So, these next chapters will summarize how God worked in people's lives throughout the pages of Scripture. We will compare the biblical record with recent claims and current needs to see how well they correspond.

GOD AFFLICTED

God physically afflicted on numerous occasions. That true aspect of God's justice frequently escapes our attention.

God brought a crushing blow to the Egyptians when they refused to let the Jews return to Palestine.

Now it came about at midnight that the Lord struck all the first-born in the land of Egypt, from the first-born of Pharaoh who sat on his throne to the first-born of the captive who was in the dungeon, and all the first-born of cattle. And Pharaoh arose in the night, he and all his servants and all the Egyptians; and there was a great cry in Egypt, for there was no home where there was not someone dead. [Exodus 12:29-30]

Literally thousands of first-born lost their lives as a punishment for a nation's disobedience.

God is not always easy on His own, either. Nadab and Abihu, the sons of Aaron, were new to the ministry. In their youthful service they offered before the Lord strange fire, which He had not commanded them to do. Instantly, fire came down from the Lord's presence and engulfed them (Leviticus 10:1-2). They died on the spot as a severe warning to the nation about the seriousness of sin.

One of the least-known facts of the Old Testament is that Ezekiel became a widower in the midst of his prophetic ministry.

Son of man, behold, I am about to take from you the desire of your eyes with a blow; but you shall not mourn, and you shall not weep, and your tears shall not come. Groan silently; make no mourning for the dead. Bind on your turban, and put your shoes on your feet, and do not cover your mustache, and do not eat the bread of men. So I spoke to the people in the morning, and in the evening my wife died. And in the morning I did as I was commanded. [Ezekiel 24:16-18]

She expired by the hand of God so that Ezekiel could be a model of mourning for Israel. As he sorrowed over the death of his wife, so they were to sorrow over their sin and God's judgment on the nation.

HEALING METHODS VARIED

God not only afflicted but also healed. No one can accuse the Lord of having one favorite healing technique. The means varied widely.

For instance, Moses prayed that Miriam would be healed of leprosy (Numbers 12:13). Seven days later (all spent outside the camp) Miriam returned healed to join the assembly again.

Nebuchadnezzar was healed seven years after God afflicted him—according to God's promised time schedule (Daniel 4:28-37).

The Syrian general Naaman emerged after seven dips in the Jordan to discover his leprosy had departed (2 Kings 5:1-14).

A healing occurred in the Judea wilderness.

Then they set out from Mount Hor by the way of the Red Sea, to go around the land of Edom; and the people became impatient because of the journey. And the people spoke against God and Moses, "Why have you brought us up out of Egypt to die in the wilderness? For there is no food and no water, and we loathe this miserable food." And the Lord sent fiery serpents among the people and they bit the people, so that many people of Israel died. So the people came to Moses and said, "We have sinned, because we have spoken against the Lord and you;

intercede with the Lord, that He may remove the serpents from us."
And Moses interceded for the people. Then the Lord said to Moses,
"Make a fiery serpent, and set it on a standard; and it shall come about,
that everyone who is bitten, when he looks at it, he shall live." And
Moses made a bronze serpent and set it on the standard; and it came
about, that if a serpent bit any man, when he looked to the bronze
serpent, he lived. [Numbers 21:4-9]

There seems to have been no Old Testament norm for a
healing method that God consistently favored.

SIN-RELATED SICKNESS

Some physical affliction was directly given because of personal
sin, although the person afflicted was not always the sinner.

Surprisingly, it seems that when affliction would be most
appropriately inflicted, it was withheld. After Aaron led the
nation into idolatrous worship, the Lord smote the people but
not Aaron (Exodus 32:35).

On other occasions the one who sinned received God's physical chastisement. Miriam was struck with leprosy for questioning
Moses' leadership (Numbers 12:1-15), and Korah died in his
rebellion against Moses (Numbers 16:1-50).

Even one who did not sin sometimes was the subject of God's
affliction. Most prominent was the child born out of David and
Bathsheba's immoral relationship (2 Samuel 12:1-23).

UNEXPLAINABLE SICKNESS

Many cases of unaccountable illness are found in the Old
Testament. They seemingly have nothing to do with sin or even
a known disease.

Mephibosheth is an example. As a baby he was dropped by his
nurse and remained lame for life (2 Samuel 4:4). Another
memorable occasion is the death of the Shunammite's son
(2 Kings 4:18-37). That instance had a pleasant ending because
Elijah then raised him from the dead.

GOD HEALED UNBELIEVERS

It was not even necessary to have a saving relationship with
God to be healed. Most notable are the healings of a Syrian
general (2 Kings 5:1-14) and a Babylonian King (Daniel
4:28-37). God healed whom He would.

GOD RESTORED LIFE

In the entire Old Testament, only three people were restored to life from the dead. The Zarephath widow's son was healed through the hand of Elijah (1 Kings 17:17-24). Elisha raised the Shunammite's son (2 Kings 4:18-37).

The third instance is unforgettable.

And Elisha died, and they buried him. Now the bands of the Moabites would invade the land in the spring of the year. And as they were burying a man, behold, they saw a marauding band; and they cast the man into the grave of Elisha. And when the man touched the bones of Elisha he revived and stood up on his feet. [2 Kings 13:20-21]

Needless to say, that was a one-of-a-kind resurrection.

SAINTS WERE SICK

Believers were not immune to physical infirmities. Isaac (Genesis 27:1) and Jacob (Genesis 48:1) became sick and died.

Job was severly smitten with boils (Job 2:7). Read Job 2:13; 3:24; 7:5, 14; 13:28; 16:8, 16; 19:17; 30:17, and 33:21 to see how seriously ill Job became. But in the end God healed him (42:10).

SUMMING IT UP

That's the revealed record:

- Saints suffered
- God afflicted
- Healing methods varied
- Unbelievers recovered
- Sinners went physically unpunished
- The innocent were struck
- Satan was insignificant
- Resurrections were rare
- Faith requirements are never mentioned

What can we conclude from those facts? Basically this: God's special interventions during the thousand years between Moses (1400 B.C.) and Malachi (400 B.C.) fall shockingly short of most people's expectations.

✦ 3 ✦

The Gospel Healing Record

A well-known collection of records begins:

Here they are! The largest, the longest, the deepest, the highest, the
fastest, the fattest, the oldest, the newest, the most startling . . . the
most spectacular . . . the most incredible . . . packed with fantastic
facts and fully documented fascinating figures . . . here it is.[1]

What book is it? *The Guinness Book of World Records!*
However, an introduction to Christ's healing ministry reads
with even greater superlatives:

And there were also many other things which Jesus did, which if they
were written in detail, I suppose that even the world itself would not
contain the books which were written. [John 21:25]

Webster's *New International Dictionary* defines *unique* as "being without a like or equal; single in kind or excellence." No

1. Norris McWhirter and Ross McWhirter, *Guinness Book of World
Records* (New York: Bantam, 1977), p. 1.

other word so accurately portrays Christ's miracles of healing.

At no other time in human history were so many people healed from such a multitude of diseases in so short a time as during Christ's public ministry. History has not repeated itself. Christ's healing ministry was truly *unique* and remains unequaled.

REASONS FOR HEALING

Various reasons existed for Christ's healing ministry, all of which contributed to the authentication of the person of Jesus as the true Messiah. The healing miracles were never performed merely for their physical benefit, as can be seen from these New Testament passages.

Matthew 8:17—A preview fulfillment of the messianic prophecy in Isaiah 53:4.

Matthew 9:6 (also Mark 2:10, Luke 5:24)—That people would know that Christ had the authority to forgive sins.

Matthew 11:2-19 (also Luke 7:18-23)—To authenticate the messianic ministry for the imprisoned John (cf. Isaiah 35).

Matthew 12:15-21—A preview fulfillment of the messianic prophecy in Isaiah 42:1-4.

John 9:3—That the works of God might be displayed in Christ.

John 11:4—For the glory of God through Christ.

John 20:30-31—That men would believe that Jesus is the Christ.

Acts 2:22—God's authentication of Christ.

HEALING HAD PURPOSE

Although Jesus' miracles were abundant, He did not perform them indiscriminately. He did not always heal everyone who needed healing (John 5:3-5); neither did He perform signs on request (Matthew 12:38-40) nor use His powers to avoid the cross (26:52-53). Miracles were always directed toward the purposes documented above.

HEALING WAS IMMEDIATE

With three exceptions, all of Christ's healings were instantaneous. No recuperative period was needed; the afflicted were immediately returned to complete health. There were no relapses or misunderstandings about being healed. "But in order that you may know that the Son of Man has authority on earth to forgive sins"—then He said to the paralytic—'Rise, take up your bed, and go home'" (Matthew 9:6-7).

The three delays in healing involved *minutes* only, but the men involved were totally healed.

And they came to Bethsaida. And they brought a blind man to Him, and entreated Him to touch him. And taking the blind man by the hand, He brought him out of the village; and after spitting on his eyes, and laying His hands upon him, He asked him, "Do you see anything?" And he looked up and said, "I see men, for I am seeing them like trees, walking about." Then again He laid His hands upon his eyes; and he looked intently and was restored, and began to see everything clearly. And He sent him to his home saying, "Do not even enter the village." [Mark 8:22-26]

HEALINGS WERE ABUNDANT

Jesus' miracles were abundant and unlimited in number and scope. "The multitude marveled as they saw the dumb speaking, the crippled restored, and the lame walking, and the blind seeing; and they glorified the God of Israel" (Matthew 15:31).

Jesus never set special times or locations for healing. He healed in the course of His Palestinian travels. His attendants never selected out of the suffering masses only those few who would actually see Him, but rather He healed all who came.

HEALING IN ABSENTIA

Jesus' physical presence was unnecessary for healing to occur. He merely thought or spoke the word and healing was accomplished. A centurion's slave (Matthew 8:5-13) and a Canaanite's daughter (Matthew 15:21-28) received their healing in that way, as did the son of a Capernaum official.

The royal official said to Him, "Sir, come down before my child dies." Jesus said to him, "Go your way; your son lives." The man believed the word that Jesus spoke to him, and he started off. And as he was now going down, his slaves met him, saying that his son was living. So he inquired of them the hour when he began to get better. They said therefore to him, "Yesterday at the seventh hour the fever left him." So the father knew that it was at that hour in which Jesus said to him, "Your son lives"; and he himself believed, and his whole household. [John 4:49-53]

HEALING METHODS VARIED

As with Old Testament healings, Jesus used a variety of healing methods. Because it was the power of God that healed, there was nothing magical or cure-producing in the method itself.

1. Christ touched (Matthew 8:15).
2. Christ spoke (John 5:8-9).
3. The afflicted touched Christ's cloak (Matthew 9:20-22).
4. Christ used spittle (Mark 8:22-26).
5. Christ plugged a man's ears with His fingers and placed spittle on his tongue (Mark 7:33-35).
6. Christ anointed with clay (John 9:6).

JESUS APPROVED DOCTORS

Jesus recognized the normal means of physical healing—a doctor and medicine. Not once did he demean the medical profession. One day He announced, "It is not those who are healthy who need a physician, but those who are sick" (Matthew 9:12). He approvingly told of the Samaritan who used oil, wine, and bandages to help the abandoned Jew (Luke 10:25-37).

HEALING FOR GOD'S GLORY

Although sickness can result directly from personal sin, as evidenced in the Old Testament, nowhere in the gospel accounts is sickness attributed directly to personal sin. However, it is stated twice that sickness occurred so that God could be glorified.

Jesus was approached one day by Martha and Mary and asked to heal their brother, Lazarus. He responded, "This sickness is not unto death, but for the glory of God, that the Son of God may be glorified by it" (John 11:4).

CHRIST'S HEALING MINISTRY WAS UNIQUE

It is stated emphatically that in previous history there was never a healing ministry like Christ's: "And as they were going out, behold, a dumb man, demon-possessed, was brought to Him. And after the demon was cast out, the dumb man spoke; and the multitudes marveled, saying, 'Nothing like this was ever seen in Israel'" (Matthew 9:32-33).

JESUS SHUNNED ACCLAIM

Jesus went out of His way to avoid public approval or reward for His healing miracles. In Luke 10:20 the disciples were told explicitly not to rejoice in the power they had been given but to rejoice in the fact that their names were recorded in heaven.

Christ never sought fame and fortune through healing. For a while He drew large crowds who heard His kingdom message, but later they crucified Him in spite of all the miracles.

HEALINGS WERE UNDENIABLE

The spectator reaction to Christ's healings was phenomenal. Everyone, including His enemies, was amazed, astounded, and unable to deny or discredit the miracles.

The most amazing statement affirming Christ's ministry came from the Pharisees and priests.

Therefore the chief priests and the Pharisees convened a council, and were saying, "What are we doing? For this man is performing many signs. If we let Him go on like this, all men will believe in Him, and the Romans will come and take away both our place and our nation." [John 11:47-48]

REACTIONS WERE WIDESPREAD

The reaction to Christ's healings was widespread. Mark 1:45 describes how the news of Christ's healing ministry spread to such an extent that He could no longer enter a city without being mobbed. Even though He remained in unpopulated areas, they came to Him from *everywhere*.

HEALING DID NOT SAVE

Christ's miracles were undeniable (John 3:2), but they did not necessarily lead to faith. For example, consider Chorazin, Bethsaida, and Capernaum.

I say to you, it will be more tolerable in that day for Sodom, than for that city. Woe to you, Chorazin! Woe to you, Bethsaida! For if the miracles had been performed in Tyre and Sidon which occurred in you, they would have repented long ago, sitting in sackcloth and ashes. But it will be more tolerable for Tyre and Sidon in the judgment, than for you. And you, Capernaum, will not be exalted to heaven, will you? You will be brought down to Hades! [Luke 10:12-15]

FAITH NOT NECESSARY

A personal faith was *not* a necessary requirement for healing. It is obvious that Lazarus (John 11), Jairus's daughter (Matthew 9), and the widow's son (Luke 7) were incapable of displaying faith. Yet, they were raised from the dead.

Furthermore, wherever Jesus healed the multitudes it can be assumed that most, if not all, were unbelievers.

And it came about while He was on the way to Jerusalem, that He was passing between Samaria and Galilee. And as He entered a certain village, ten leprous men who stood at a distance met Him; and they raised their voices, saying, "Jesus, Master, have mercy on us!" And when He saw them, He said to them, "Go and show yourselves to the priests." And it came about that as they were going, they were cleansed. Now one of them, when he saw that he had been healed, turned back, glorifying God with a loud voice, and he fell on his face at His feet, giving thanks to Him. And he was a Samaritan. And Jesus answered and said, "Were there not ten cleansed? But the nine—where are they? Was no one found who turned back to give glory to God, except this foreigner?" And He said to him, "Rise, and go your way; your faith has made you well." [Luke 17:11-19]

ANOTHER'S FAITH HONORED

At times, Christ healed when faith was displayed by someone other than the one afflicted. Note especially Matthew 17:19-20. The disciples had been unable to cast out a demon and came to Jesus privately for further instruction. He informed them that it was because of their lack of faith. The parallel passage in Mark (9:29) adds that prayer would have been successful. Those who claim that a person can remain unhealed because of his own lack of faith need to be alerted. In this case the deficient faith belonged to the would-be healers.

HEALINGS WERE NOT PREARRANGED

Jesus healed from the beginning of His ministry (Matthew 4:23-25) to the end (John 11:1-44). Often He approached the person, as He did the lame man at the pool of Bethesda (John 5:1-9). Furthermore, Jesus always healed during the normal course of His daily ministry.

> And as Jesus passed on from there, two blind men followed Him crying out and saying, "Have mercy on us, Son of David!" And after He had come into the house, the blind men came up to Him, and Jesus said to them, "Do you believe that I am able to do this?" They said to Him, "Yes, Lord." Then He touched their eyes, saying, "Be it done to you according to your faith." [Matthew 9:27-29]

SATAN CAUSED SICKNESS

Not all sickness is directly caused by Satan or demons, but those who are possessed by demons are liable to have physical infirmities. A classic example is in Luke 13:10-17, where a woman bound by Satan (possibly through a demon) was doubled over for eighteen years.

HEAVENLY HEALING POWER

Because Christ had voluntarily abandoned the *independent* exercise of His divine attributes, His healing power came from God the Father; it was not self-generated:

> He cast out demons by the Spirit of God (Matthew 12:28).
> "And the power of the Lord was present for Him to perform healing" (Luke 5:17).
> He cast out demons by the finger of God (Luke 11:20).
> "The Son can do nothing of Himself" (John 5:19).
> "Signs which God performed through Him" (Acts 2:22).
> Christ healed because God was with Him (Acts 10:38).

HEALING BY THE DISCIPLES

People other than Christ performed healings in the gospel accounts. For example, the disciples were sent by Jesus Himself on their preaching and healing excursions (Matt. 10:1-15).

Seventy other disciples were similarly commissioned by the Lord to preach and heal (Luke 10:1-16).

The evidence is convincing. Christ's healings were:

- undeniable
- spectacular
- overwhelming
- abundant
- awesome

No one before or since has even fractionally approached the power of Jesus Christ to heal. He was unique.

However, God's healing power did not stop with His Son but continued through the apostles. The Acts and epistles tell that story.

♦ 4 ♦

The Healing Record
in Acts and the Epistles

The Lord Jesus Christ told His disciples in the Upper Room, "Truly, truly, I say to you, he who believes in Me, the works that I do shall he do also" (John 14:12).

Jesus' word was authoritative. Because He had promised, He would surely fulfill His word.

The apostles had briefly seen God's healing power work through them before Christ died (Matthew 10:1-15; Luke 10:1-16). After Christ ascended to the right hand of God the Father, the apostles became His chief representatives on earth and the ones through whom God worked miraculously.

He kept His promise. As Jesus had been authenticated by miracles (Acts 2:22), so too were the apostles (Hebrews 2:1-4). The book of Acts and the apostles' letters bear record.

THE ACTS OF THE APOSTLES

HEALING TECHNIQUES VARIED

The healing techniques varied in Acts as they did in the Old Testament and the gospels.

1. By command (Acts 3:6)
2. By being in the healer's shadow (Acts 5:15)
3. By touching a cloth from the healer's body (Acts 19:11-12)
4. By prayer and the laying on of hands (Acts 28:8-9)

HEALING WAS IMMEDIATE

In Acts the afflicted were immediately restored to full health. That is, the healings were instantaneous, with no recuperative period required.

And at Lystra there was sitting a certain man, without strength in his feet, lame from his mother's womb, who had never walked. This man was listening to Paul as he spoke, who, when he had fixed his gaze upon him, and had seen that he had faith to be made well, said with a loud voice, "Stand upright on your feet." And he leaped up and began to walk. [Acts 14:8-10]

UNBELIEVERS WERE HEALED

As in Christ's ministry, saving faith in Jesus Christ was not a necessary requirement for healing.

And the multitudes with one accord were giving attention to what was said by Philip, as they heard and saw the signs which he was performing. For in the case of many who had unclean spirits, they were coming out of them shouting with a loud voice; and many who had been paralyzed and lame were healed. [Acts 8:6-7]

FAITH OF THE AFFLICTED HONORED

At times, the faith of the afflicted was commended. Peter delivered this commendation: "And on the basis of faith in His name, it is the name of Jesus which has strengthened this man whom you see and know; and the faith which comes through Him has given him this perfect health in the presence of you all" (Acts 3:16).

Yet at other times a personal faith was not necessarily required of the afflicted. "And Peter said to him, 'Aeneas, Jesus Christ heals you; arise, and make your bed.' And immediately he arose" (Acts 9:34).

HEALINGS WERE UNDENIABLE

The miracles of healing were undeniable—even by the Sanhedrin.

> But when they had ordered them to go aside out of the Council, they began to confer with one another, saying, "What shall we do with these men? For the fact that a noteworthy miracle has taken place through them is apparent to all who live in Jerusalem, and we cannot deny it. But in order that it may not spread any further among the people, let us warn them to speak no more to any man in this name." [Acts 4:15-17]

SIN-RELATED SICKNESS

Sometimes God afflicted people because of personal sin. He afflicted Ananias and Sapphira after they lied to the Holy Spirit.

> And as he heard these words, Ananias fell down and breathed his last; and great fear came upon all who heard of it. . . . And she fell immediately at his feet, and breathed her last; and the young men came in and found her dead, and they carried her out and buried her beside her husband. [Acts 5:5, 10]

LIFE RESTORED

Two people were raised from the dead—Dorcas (Acts 9:30-43) and Eutychus (Acts 20:9-12).

HEALING IN ABSENTIA

God worked so powerfully through Paul that cloths touched by him could bring healing without his presence. "And God was performing extraordinary miracles by the hands of Paul, so that handkerchiefs or aprons were even carried from his body to the sick, and the diseases left them and the evil spirits went out" (Acts 19:11-12).

THE APOSTOLIC EPISTLES

PURPOSE OF HEALING

Signs, miracles, and wonders were used to authenticate the apostles and their ministry (Romans 15:18-19; 2 Corinthians 12:12; Hebrews 2:4).

Spectacular supernatural healings were among the signs displayed by the apostles and by those to whom they personally ministered. Whether the apostles themselves or those they ministered to did the signs, those signs were to attest the authority of the apostles as revealers of truth (see Acts 2:42-43).

If all nonapostolic Christians are supposed to perform such deeds, such deeds could not have served as the signs of apostleship (see 2 Corinthians 12:12). The signs attested the apostles' words as having equal authority with those of Jesus Himself, for He had chosen them as His spokesmen (see Matthew 10:11-15, 20, 40; 1 Corinthians 14:37).

HEALING DECLINED

Paul's frequency of healing declined with the passing of time.

> Galatians 4:13-15—Paul was ill
> 2 Corinthians 12:7-10—Paul was afflicted
> Philippians 2:25-30—Epaphroditus was ill
> 1 Timothy 5:23—Timothy was ill
> 2 Timothy 4:20—Trophimus was ill

Healing is noticeable in the Old Testament, overwhelming in the gospels, frequent in Acts, and negligible in the epistles. The apostolic age ended and miraculous healing by direct human intervention ceased.

MEDICINE APPROVED

Paul recognized and recommended medicine. He recommended wine to settle Timothy's stomach: "No longer drink water exclusively, but use a little wine for the sake of your stomach and your frequent ailments" (1 Timothy 5:23).

SIN-RELATED SICKNESS

James 5:14-20 outlines the biblical response for severe or untimely physical infirmities that could have their source in God's chastisement for personal sin. This passage is so important that we will discuss it fully in a later chapter. It is safe to say that healings became less noticeable with time, even in the apostolic era. But did such healings end with the apostles' deaths?

◆ 5 ◆

Is Healing in the Atonement?

Several years ago I was browsing through some commentaries at my favorite bookstore in Columbus, Ohio. A dear lady whom I had recently visited in the hospital entered and walked toward me. Greeting her, I remarked how well she looked. She responded, "By His stripes I have been healed—praise God there is healing in Christ's atonement."

Immediately I decided that the bookstore was no place for a theology discussion. I didn't want to dampen her new joy nor did I want to rob her of her confidence that somehow God had been involved in her physical restoration. However, her proof texts—Isaiah 53:5 and 1 Peter 2:24—just did not describe what had happened to her.

I wondered where she had got those proof texts. Perhaps she had read a faith healer's explanation of Isaiah 53 or listened to a faith healer on television. A friend or neighbor may have told her.

It could be that you have had the same experience. Perhaps the truth of Christ's healing through the atonement has puzzled you. We need to look at Isaiah 53 and other related passages to answer such questions as, Is there healing in the atonement? If there is, What kind? How much? and, When do I get it?

THE ATONEMENT

Isaiah 53 is really the heart of anyone's healing theology. It is the bedrock upon which our expectations for restored health rest. The "Magna Charta" of God's healing promises focuses on Christ's sacrificial death at Calvary.

The atonement is first found in Scripture in the sacrificial system of the book of Leviticus, which paints the Day of Atonement portrait. It was the one day of the year that the high priest entered the Holy of Holies and approached the Ark of the Covenant to sprinkle blood to atone for the sins of Israel.

Aaron was the brother of Moses and the first high priest. Leviticus 16:3 tells us that Aaron entered the Holy Place with a bull for an offering—was it a *sin* or a *sick* offering? Obviously it was a sin offering.

- Two male goats stand for a *sin* offering. Aaron offers a bull for a *sin* offering—first for himself and his household (vv. 5-6).
- "Aaron shall offer the bull of the *sin* offering" (v. 11).
- "He shall make atonement for the holy place, because of the impurities of the sons of Israel, and because of their transgressions in regard to all their *sins*" (v. 16).
- "Aaron shall lay both of his hands on the head of the live goat, and confess over it all the iniquities of the sons of Israel and all their transgressions in regard to all their *sins*" (v. 21).
- Aaron shall have this as a permanent statute to make annual atonement for the sons of Israel because of all their *sins* (v. 34).

The picture that Moses portrayed was fulfilled in Jesus Christ who died for our *sins*—not our sicknesses.

Moses instituted the Day of Atonement by the authority of God about 1400 B.C. Hundreds of years later (about 700 B.C.),

Isaiah wrote about a coming servant who would be "the atonement."

In the book of Hebrews (the "Leviticus" of the New Testament) you can appreciate the unity of Scripture. When the final atonement was offered, Christ was both the high priest and the sacrifice.

> But when Christ appeared as a high priest of the good things to come, He entered through the greater and more perfect tabernacle, not made with hands, that is to say, not of this creation; and not through the blood of goats and calves, but through His own blood, He entered the holy place once for all, having obtained eternal redemption. [Hebrews 9:11-12]

Jesus Christ as God incarnate was the Lamb slain for the sins of the world.

Hebrews 10 contains several passages that relate to the atonement's fulfillment in Jesus Christ. "Then He said, 'Behold, I have come to do Thy will.' He takes away the first in order to establish the second. By this will we have been sanctified through the offering of the body of Jesus Christ once for all" (Hebrews 10:9-10).

Year after year the high priest had to first make atonement for himself and his family and then for the nation. But Christ had to sacrifice only once. That is what Isaiah 53 anticipated. "But He, having offered one sacrifice for sins for all time, sat down at the right hand of God. . . . For by one offering He has perfected for all time those who are sanctified" (Hebrews 10:12, 14).

Both Leviticus and Hebrews demonstrate that in the mind of God the atonement primarily dealt with sin, not sickness. It had everything to do with our sin problem and the redemption that we needed to remove sin, that we might stand before a holy God. The due penalty for sin was paid; it was poured out upon Jesus Christ. Thus, the major emphasis of Isaiah 53 is salvation.

TEXTUAL COMMENTS ON ISAIAH 53

Isaiah 53:4-6 raises the question, What does the prophet promise about physical restoration?

> Surely our griefs He Himself bore,
> And our sorrows He carried;
> Yet we ourselves esteemed Him stricken,
> Smitten of God, and afflicted.
> But He was pierced through for our transgressions,
> He was crushed for our iniquities;
> The chastening for our well-being fell upon Him,
> And by His scourging we are healed.
> All of us like sheep have gone astray,
> Each of us has turned to his own way;
> But the Lord has caused the iniquity of us all
> To fall on Him.

The Hebrew words translated "griefs" and "sorrows" in Isaiah 53:4 can refer legitimately to either physical or mental pain and spiritual problems. Those who say that the language refers only to physical problems should more accurately say that the words *may* refer to physical problems.

However, words are always used in a context and with an intended meaning by the author. Normally, the surrounding context indicates what the author meant by the words he used.

Iniquity is used four times in Isaiah 53 and identifies the passage's major emphasis. In verse 5, Christ was crushed for our *iniquities;* so that, in verse 6, the Lord has caused the iniquity of us all to fall on Him; in verse 11, that He will bear their iniquities, and in verse 12, that He Himself bore the *sins* of many. The primary thrust of Isaiah 53 is on the spiritual and the eternal effects of sin, not on its physical and immediate effects upon the body.

In verse 4 we read that He bore our griefs and carried our sorrows. Isaiah uses those same verbs in verses 11 and 12. As we compare verses 3 and 4 with verses 11 and 12, we see that the primary thrust is salvation.

We find that He will bear our iniquities (v. 11) and that "He Himself bore the sins of many" (v. 12). Hebrews 9:28 makes the grand allusion: "Christ also having been offered once to bear the sins of many."

We will discover that there is also a secondary reference to the physical effect that sin can produce upon the body. Yet, Isaiah 53 needs to be understood primarily in terms of God's redemptive program.

THEOLOGICAL COMMENTS ON ISAIAH 53

Let us consider some clarifying theological observations from other portions of Scripture.

First, our present body is corruptible; that is, it will degenerate until we will die. The physical will be separated from the spiritual. But the good news for believers is that one day we will put on the incorruptible—a form that will remain constant, pure, and without sin for all eternity. "And not only this, but also we ourselves, having the first fruits of the Spirit, even we ourselves groan within ourselves, waiting eagerly for our adoption as sons, the redemption of our body" (Romans 8:23).

We only have the firstfruits of the Spirit. By analogy, we redemptively have only the firstfruits. We won't begin to see what God is going to do in us until we leave this world and our bodies are ushered into heaven.

We now groan within ourselves, eagerly waiting for our adoption as sons and the redemption of our *bodies*. It will be fantastic. Afflictions and wheelchairs will be no more because the moral source of sickness—sin—will be no more.

Second, Christ died for our sins. The gospel is immediately good news about our sin problem, but not so with our physical problems. You can read about that in these passages: Matthew 1:21, John 1:29, Romans 1:16, 1 Corinthians 15:1-3, Ephesians 1:7, Colossians 1:14, Hebrews 9, and 1 John 3:5.

Next, Christ was made sin and not sickness. Second Corinthians 5 is very important because it talks about the ministry of reconciliation. "He made Him who knew no sin to be sin on our behalf, that we might become the righteousness of God in Him" (2 Corinthians 5:21). Christ was never made sickness.

Fourth, Christ forgave our sins, not our sicknesses. John says: "I am writing to you, little children, because your sins are forgiven you for His name's sake" (1 John 2:12).

Fifth, Christ gave Himself primarily for our sins and not for our sicknesses. "Grace to you and peace from God our Father, and the Lord Jesus Christ, who gave Himself for our sins, that He might deliver us out of this present evil age, according to the will of our God and Father" (Galatians 1:3-4).

Next, the Bible teaches that if a person is truly saved, he cannot lose his salvation (John 10:28-29; Philippians 1:6; Jude 24). Now observe the logical line of thought necessary to follow if physical healing is as much in the atonement for today as is redemption. If a person is truly saved he cannot lose his salvation (John 5:24). God has given salvation through no merit of our own—through no price that we paid. Since that is true, if physical healing shares in the atonement, as does spiritual healing, we should not lose our physical health.

But is that what really happens? No! The Scripture says we all must die (Hebrews 9:27)! We could look at such godly examples as Abraham, Isaac, Daniel, Paul, and Timothy to show that God's greatest saints were sick. They also eventually died.

Seventh, as true believers we are assured of our salvation but have no guarantee of our physical life or our health.

> Come now, you who say, "Today or tomorrow, we shall go to such and such a city, and spend a year there and engage in business and make a profit." Yet you do not know what your life will be like tomorrow. You are just a vapor that appears for a little while and then vanishes away. [James 4:13-14]

There is no guarantee that any of us will be here tomorrow. But there is every guarantee that if we place our faith in Jesus Christ we will still be His sons and daughters.

If healing is in the atonement and if it applies physically today, those who would ask by faith for physical healing and are not healed have no logical right to be assured of their salvation. God says if we are saved, we have every right to believe in our salvation. And if physical healing were in the atonement and we ask to be healed and are not, not only do we lose our assurance of the physical, but we would also lose our assurance of the spiritual. Fortunately, those contradictions can only be produced if we have taken a wrong approach to what the atonement is all about.

Eighth, if physical healing in the atonement were to be applied today, logically, eternal life must also be applied today.

But again, death becomes our great nemesis and stumbling block to that proposed truth. We are all going to die (Hebrews 9:27). Death will not be abolished in human existence until the eternal state commences. Therefore, whatever physical benefits are found in the atonement, they will not be fully experienced until eternity—until we are in the presence of God.

The Bible does not teach anywhere that sickness needs atonement, but it does teach everywhere that sinners require atonement for forgiveness of their sin.

If Christ paid the penalty for our sin and we are still sinning, what ought to be the experience in the physical realm? Total health or impaired health? Just as we have impaired spiritual health, so we will continue to have impaired physical health until the experience of sin is removed. That won't happen until death or until the Lord comes!

In reality, Christ paid the penalty for sin but He did not remove sin from the life of the believer. Christ cared for the cause of sickness; that is, the cause of sickness in its moral sense. But He did not remove sickness from the life experience of believers because He did not remove sin from their life experience.

If the conclusions we have reached in Isaiah 53 and elsewhere are true, the New Testament will verify them. The Scriptures are marvelously unified and will not contradict themselves.

Isaiah 53 is not without its New Testament witness. Philip encountered the Ethiopian eunuch reading Isaiah 53 (Acts 8:28, 32-33). When the eunuch asked Philip for an explanation, he preached Jesus to him (Acts 8:35). Apparently, the eunuch invited Christ to be his personal Savior and Lord because he next asked about baptism. The point we should note is this: both Philip and the Ethiopian eunuch understood Isaiah 53 to be dealing with sin, not sickness.

MATTHEW ON ISAIAH 53

Matthew 8-9 records the most concentrated period of healing in the gospel record. Look at Matthew 8:14-17.

> And when Jesus had come to Peter's home, He saw his mother-in-law lying sick in bed with a fever. And He touched her hand, and the fever left her; and she arose, and waited on Him. And when evening had come, they brought to Him many who were demon-possessed; and He cast out the spirits with a word, and healed all who were ill in order that what was spoken through Isaiah the prophet might be fulfilled, saying, "He Himself took our infirmities, and carried away our diseases."

Our task is to understand what Matthew meant in that passage. A cursory reading of the English text does not provide that clarification. It is a very difficult passage and unless we more fully understand its language, we will never understand what our Lord was trying to teach.

The Greek words translated "took" and "carry" are different from the corresponding Greek words that are used in the Greek translation (the Septuagint) of Isaiah 53. The translators used two Greek words to translate Isaiah 53:4. However, Matthew used two other Greek words in 8:17 than the Old Testament translators used in Isaiah 53:4. There is a good reason for the change.

The words in Matthew 8 mean "to take away from," not "to bear." That difference helps us to understand what Jesus was teaching. The words used to translate Isaiah 53:4 mean "to sacrificially bear"; thus, the idea that "He took our sins upon Him."

However, Matthew is saying here that Christ took away their sicknesses. Christ did not bear in a substitutionary sense the sickness of Peter's mother-in-law. He didn't say, "Move fever from her into Me." He just touched her and it was gone. Neither did He bear the afflictions of those who were ill nor the spirits of those who were possessed (8:16). Later He would bear sin on Calvary, but at this point He had only taken away their sicknesses.

This next thought is important. What Christ did at Calvary occurred several years after His healing ministry at Capernaum as reported in Matthew 8. There is absolutely no effectual relationship between what Christ did in Capernaum and His atonement on the cross at Calvary. Matthew employed a normal illustrative use of the Old Testament. He found a point of continuity, a point of identity between Isaiah 53 and Christ's healing ministry in Capernaum.

Matthew 2:14-15 illustrates that by quoting Hosea 11:1.

And he arose and took the Child and His mother by night, and departed for Egypt; and was there until the death of Herod, that what was spoken by the Lord through the prophet might be fulfilled, saying, "Out of Egypt did I call My Son."

Matthew is talking about the childhood of our Lord and Herod's desire to put Him to death. Hosea was talking about the redemption of Israel out of the bondage of Egypt about 1440 B.C. What relation is there between Israel and Christ? None directly, perhaps, but it is true they both were in Egypt and God redeemed them both from Egypt. That is, He brought them out of bondage and back into the land of Palestine. That is the point of identity and how the prophecy of Hosea 11:1 was used by Matthew.

Here is another way to look at it. Matthew 8 is to Isaiah 53 (in terms of its analogy) as Matthew 17 (the transfiguration of Christ) is to Revelation 19. It is merely a preview, just as Matthew 8 is a preview of the coming eternal kingdom that will be free of sin and sickness.

There is no more of a basis for believing that because Christ cared for physical affliction at Calvary there is now no sickness than there is to suggest that because Christ bore our sins at Calvary there is now no sin. As long as sin exists, the moral basis for sickness will continue. You and I, as believers, have the potential for incurable physical distress. What Christ did at Capernaum or Calvary will not eliminate sickness in the life of the believer. Matthew 8 is a preview of Christ's messianic ministry that authenticated His claim to be the Son of God. At Capernaum He merely removed sickness. Now before we draw some final conclusions, let's look at Peter's use of Isaiah 53.

PETER ON ISAIAH 53

For you have been called for this purpose, since Christ also suffered for you, leaving you an example for you to follow in His steps, who committed no sin, nor was any deceit found in His mouth: and while being reviled, He did not revile in return; while suffering, He uttered no threats, but kept entrusting Himself to Him who judges righteously; and He Himself bore our sins in His body on the cross, that we might die to sin and live to righteousness; for by His wounds you were healed. [1 Pet. 2:21-24]

Did Christ die for our sins or for our sicknesses? The context demands that we understand that Christ died for our sins. A question often asked is, What does the word for *wound* mean, or "by His stripes"? The word translated "scourging" in the NASB, "stripes" in the KJV, and "wounds" in the NIV is best translated from the Hebrew text in Isaiah 53:5 as "wounds from physical abuse." That is how Peter understood Isaiah. In context, it is speaking not primarily of the scourging that Christ received in a preparatory way at the hands of the soldiers, but rather of the totality of the excruciating suffering He endured at Calvary. The beatings and torments that He suffered before He was nailed to the cross were nothing by comparison to the agony He suffered at Calvary when He bore the sins of the world.

The psalmist wrote:

> I am poured out like water,
> And all my bones are out of joint;
> My heart is like wax;
> It is melted within me.
> My strength is dried up like a potsherd,
> And my tongue cleaves to my jaws;
> And Thou dost lay me in the dust of death.
> For dogs have surrounded me;
> A band of evildoers has encompassed me;
> They pierced my hands and my feet.
> I can count all my bones,
> They look, they stare at me.
>
> Psalm 22:14-17

The context in 1 Peter 2 deals with our spiritual healing and the payment for sin, not for sickness.

SUMMING IT UP

Isaiah 53 refers primarily to the atonement and its redemptive value, not its therapeutic effect in a physical sense. Three lines of evidence support that reasoning:

1. The idea of atonement in Leviticus and Hebrews is applied primarily to salvation.
2. The context of Isaiah 53 focuses primarily on the atonement's provision for sin.
3. The theological context of Christ's death and salvation is centered primarily on sin.

Isaiah 53 primarily deals with the spiritual being of man. Its major emphasis is on sin, not sickness. It focuses on the moral cause of sickness, which is sin, and not on the immediate removal of one of sin's results—sickness.

Matthew 8 is a limited and localized preview of a believer's experience in eternity, where sickness will be no more because sin will be no more. Christ did not personally bear sickness in Capernaum in a substitutionary way, but instead removed it. Matthew refers to Isaiah 53 for illustrative purposes and by no means intends it to be understood as meaning that the prophecy of Isaiah 53 was fulfilled two years before Christ went to Calvary.

First Peter 2:24 rehearses the primary redemptive implication of Isaiah 53. Christ's atoning death provided the basis for spiritual health and eternal life. Our iniquities were borne by Christ to satisfy God's righteous demand against sin. Physical health and healing are not primarily in view.

The question we asked when we began was, Is there healing in the atonement? My answer is, Yes! There is healing in the atonement, but it is never promised to believers for the present. When sin is removed, physical healing for believers will be in full, but only in the future, when our bodies have been redeemed by the power of God (Romans 8:23).

When we look at the language used, understand the context in which the above passages are found, see the complementing passages in Leviticus and Hebrews, and realize what was involved in the atonement, we can see that the atonement dealt with sin and the need to satisfy the righteous wrath of a just and holy God.

It will not be until sin is removed from our personal existence that you and I can have any hope of guaranteed physical well-being. When the full fruit of redemption is added to the present firstfruits, we will know the fullness of physical healing provided by the atonement.

James I. Packer eloquently captures the intent of Isaiah 53 with this insightful summary.

Again it is true: salvation embraces both body and soul. And there is indeed, as some put it, healing for the body in the Atonement. But, we must observe that perfect physical health is promised, not for this life, but for heaven, as part of the resurrection glory that awaits us in the day when Christ "will change our lowly body to be like his glorious body, by the power which enables him even to subject all things to himself." Full bodily well-being is set forth as a future blessing of salvation rather than a present one. What God has promised, and when he will give it, are separate questions.[1]

1. James I. Packer, "Poor Health May Be the Best Remedy," *Christianity Today*, 21 May 1982, p. 15.

✦ 6 ✦

Biblical Answers to Difficult Passages

When you were young, did your parents (or someone else you loved) ever promise you something they never provided? A fishing trip? Some money? A certain birthday gift? A trip to a ball game?

You can probably still remember your deep disappointment. Chances are you promised yourself that you would never do that to someone because you knew how much it hurt. Yet, many Christians do that very thing by misrepresenting God's promises and raising expectations that can never be realized.

An illustration of that kind of situation is found in Philip Yancey's best-seller *Where Is God When It Hurts?* This letter vividly recounts the agonizing despair that can be caused when expectations of God's blessing are not fulfilled.

Someone told me just after I became a Christian that God would heal me. This seemed too good to be true, and I didn't know if I dared believe it. But seeing nothing in the Bible that contradicted it, I began to hope, and then to believe. But my faith was shaky, and when Christians came along and said, "God doesn't heal everyone," or

"Affliction is a cross we must bear," my faith would waver. Then last fall it just seemed to die. I gave up believing God would heal me.

At that point in my life I knew I couldn't face spending the rest of my life in the wheelchair. Knowing that God had the power to heal me but wouldn't (or so I thought) made me very bitter. I would read Isaiah 53, and 1 Peter 2:24, and accuse God of holding the promise of healing before me like a piece of meat before a starving dog. He tempted me by showing the potential but never quite allowing me to reach it. This in turn produced deep guilt feelings because from the Bible I knew God was a loving God and answerable to no man. I had such a conflict in me that my mental state was precarious and I thought of suicide many times.

I began to take tranquilizers just to get through the day as my guilt and resentment built a higher and higher wall between God and me. About this time I began having headaches and problems with my eyes. An ophthalmologist could find no physical reason.

I was still praying because I knew God was alive, but I usually ended up crying and railing out at God. I'm afraid I experienced a lot of self-pity, which was very destructive. And over and over I asked God why He wouldn't heal me when it so plainly says that healing is a part of the redemption plan.[1]

There is nothing quite so cruel as giving hope for healing if the Scriptures do not really provide that hope. Thus, it is imperative to correctly interpret Scripture so that we do not create the damaging despair that we have just encountered in this touching letter.

Several passages are frequently misinterpreted by faith healers. They are wrongly used to promise the certain hope of physical healing today for everyone who believes.

EXODUS 15:26

(Exodus 23:25; Deuteronomy 7:15)

And He said, "If you will give earnest heed to the voice of the Lord your God, and do what is right in His sight, and give ear to His commandments, and keep all His statutes, I will put none of the

---

1. Philip Yancey, *Where Is God When It Hurts?* (Grand Rapids: Zondervan, 1977), pp. 151-52.

diseases on you which I have put on the Egyptians; for I, the Lord, am your healer."

Many claim that passage as a promise for today. But is it?

After Moses led the children of Israel out of Egypt and across the Red Sea, they went into the wilderness of Shur. For three days they suffered without liquid. Finally, they found water; but it was bitter and they grumbled at Moses. He prayed to God and then took a tree that the Lord showed him and threw it into the water, and the water became sweet.

In verse 26 God strongly exhorted the Jews to do what was right and to obey all of His commandments. If they did, God would not afflict them as He did the Egyptians. The Jews had a visual aid to emphasize the scope of the Lord's statement. The agonizing look on Pharaoh's face had testified of God's power to afflict.

The theological basis for this exhortation is the fact that metaphysically God is responsible for all healings regardless of the disease, the cure, or the spiritual state of the one cured. God says in Deuteronomy 32:39: "See now that I, I am He and there is no god besides Me; it is I who put to death and give life. I have wounded, and it is I who heal; and there is no one who can deliver from My hand." So to reassure the Jews, God added in Exodus 15:26, "I, the LORD, am your healer."

If the historic Exodus of the Jewish nation is followed further, we come to Deuteronomy 28, which broadly explains the subsequent history of Israel in the Old Testament. In Deuteronomy 28 God promised Israel that if she disobeyed she could expect pestilence and disease (among other things), just as she had seen forty years earlier in Egypt (Deuteronomy 28:21-22, 27, 35, 59-61).

Years later, Israel continually disobeyed and God finally judged. Examples of fulfilled judgment promised in Deuteronomy 28 include Jeremiah 14:12, 21:6; Ezekiel 5:12, 6:11; and Amos 4:9-10. Israel sinned; God judged. Psalm 106 also provides an excellent panoramic view of Israel's sin from God's viewpoint during that period.

Two matters need to be clarified. First, Exodus 15:26 makes a conditional promise to a specific group of people (Israel). Second, the promise is temporal in nature. It is conditional, not upon God's ability to heal but upon Israel's obedience.

Today God is dealing primarily not with the nation of Israel (Romans 11) but with the church, in which there is no distinction between Jew and Gentile (Galatians 3:28). Because of Israel's disobedience, God carried out His conditional promise primarily in judgment, not healing.

Furthermore, although Israel enjoyed God's blessing with regard to health, that blessing did not preclude the use of means or doctors. God appointed Levitical priests as health officers (Leviticus 13). The sanitation laws of the Levitical code provided means to health that were not practiced by the Western world until the last two centuries.

We do not currently expect any of the judgments promised to Israel (Deuteronomy 28:15-68). And because we are not enjoying any of the blessings that were enjoyed during her forty-year wilderness sojourn (such as daily rations of manna and quail in Exodus 16:1-21 or clothes and shoes that never wore out as in Deuteronomy 29:5), the conditional promise to Israel in Exodus 15:26 does not apply to the church today. God has been, is, and always will be capable of healing any disease at any time, but only according to His revealed will in Scripture. Exodus 15:26 is simply not a promise for believers today.

PSALM 103:1-3

> Bless the LORD, O my soul;
> And all that is within me, bless His holy name.
> Bless the Lord, O my soul,
> And forget none of His benefits;
> Who pardons all your iniquities;
> Who heals all your diseases.

Psalm 103 opens with a five-verse monologue by David, in which he recalls to his own soul the blessings the Lord has bestowed on him. It is a beautiful combination of both spiritual and material blessings.

The Hebrew word for *diseases* used in verse 3 appears five times in the Old Testament and always refers to physical disease. In typical Hebrew poetic parallelism David very beautifully contrasts God's spiritual blessing of pardoning iniquities with God's material blessing of physical healing. David restates here what Moses wrote in Deuteronomy 32:39: that the Lord is ultimately responsible for *all* healings.

Anyone who recovers from a physical affliction, believer or unbeliever, can thank God for the recovery. Many doctors will admit that even after the best in medical technology has been applied to the problem, it is really God who heals. David was merely rejoicing in that eternal truth.

So far as biblical history records, David never suffered from an incurable disease. He had always recovered from sickness and in each instance gave God the glory. David's life clearly demonstrates that sin can be responsible for physical ailments. Psalms 32:3-4, 38:3, and 41:4 all refer to physical symptoms stemming from a spiritual source. David, who was a man after God's heart, knew how to recognize sin, although he was not always careful to avoid it. The guilt of David's conscience produced negative physical effects. As David anguished over his sin, his body wasted away (Psalm 32:3-4), but his confession and repentance brought both spiritual and physical relief (vv. 5-7). In David's case, his guilt was primarily a spiritual problem, not physiological, although he experienced definite physical effects.

David's statement in Psalm 103:3 does not mean that God heals *all* disease. God is capable of such healing but does not always do so. David was merely rehearsing before himself the fact that God had healed all of *his* prior illnesses.

The statement also does not deny, preclude, or prohibit the use of means to attain health. David's comments are based on the fact that whatever means are used, God should be given the glory.

Therefore, what was true of David's life in Psalm 103:3 in terms of physical relief is not necessarily true (nor is it a promise of such) in any other believer's life. David himself was subject to death, slept with his fathers, and was buried in the city of David (1 Kings 2:1, 10; Acts 2:29; 13:36).

ISAIAH 35:4-5

Say to those with anxious heart,
"Take courage, fear not.
Behold, your God will come with vengeance;
The recompense of God will come,
But He will save you."
Then the eyes of the blind will be opened,
And the ears of the deaf will be unstopped.

A quick reading of Isaiah 35 will indicate that the prophet was writing about a spectacular time in the future of Israel. However, both Luke 7:18-23 and Matthew 11:2-6 record that Jesus referred to this passage when He verified His messianic authority by curing many diseases and afflictions and granting sight to many who were blind (Luke 7:21). He told John's disciples to return to him and report what they had seen. It is implied that when John heard the report he would know without doubt that Jesus was the Messiah.

It is obvious that all of Isaiah 35 was not realized during the earthly ministry of Christ. What Christ did during His ministry with regard to healing only previewed what is to come during His one-thousand-year reign in glory (Revelation 19:1—20:15).

At the end of the millennial period Christ will deliver up the kingdom to God the Father (1 Corinthians 15:24). But He must reign until He has put all His enemies under His feet; and the last enemy to be abolished is death (vv. 25-26).

When death has been abolished, it will signal the end of sin. No longer will there be a basis for sickness. Even the millennial healing ministry of the Messiah will no longer be needed. Revelation 21:4 says that no longer will there be death, mourning, crying, or pain. Referring to Genesis 3:8-22, where the curse was initiated, Revelation 22:3 reveals the reason—there will no longer be a curse.

Isaiah 35:4-5 refers primarily then to millennial conditions. Christ's healing ministry in the gospels, and specifically for the disciples of John, was a mere preview of things to come and authenticated Jesus as Messiah. It has no bearing whatsoever on our understanding of God's work of healing today other than to encourage the earnest believer by the knowledge of his future eternal relationship with God, when there will be no sin and thus no sickness.

MARK 16:9-20

Now after He had risen early on the first day of the week, He first appeared to Mary Magdalene, from whom He had cast out seven demons. She went and reported to those who had been with Him, while they were mourning and weeping. And when they heard that He was alive, and had been seen by her, they refused to believe it. And after that, He appeared in a different form to two of them, while they were walking along on their way to the country. And they went away and reported it to the others, but they did not believe them either. And afterward He appeared to the eleven themselves as they were reclining at the table; and He reproached them for their unbelief and hardness of heart, because they had not believed those who had seen Him after He had risen. And He said to them, "Go into all the world and preach the gospel to all creation. He who has believed and has been baptized shall be saved; but he who has disbelieved shall be condemned. And these signs will accompany those who have believed: in My name they will cast out demons, they will speak with new tongues; they will pick up serpents, and if they drink any deadly poison, it shall not hurt them; they will lay hands on the sick, and they will recover." So then, when the Lord Jesus had spoken to them, He was received up into heaven, and sat down at the right hand of God. And they went out and preached everywhere, while the Lord worked with them, and confirmed the word by the signs that followed.

One of the most controversial textual problems in all of the New Testament is the one dealing with the concluding verses of the gospel of Mark. There are three textual possibilities:

1. Mark 16:1-8—normal ending
2. Mark 16:1-20—longer ending
3. Mark 16:1-8—with a special addition

The problem is that Mark 16:9-20 is not present in the oldest existing Greek manuscripts (Codex Sinaiticus [c. 340] and Codex Vaticanus [c. 325-50]) or in a number of other important early manuscript witnesses to the text of the New Testament. It is the opinion of many that "on the basis of good external evidence and strong internal considerations it appears that the earliest ascertainable forms of the Gospel of Mark ended with 16:8."[2]

Neither is there conclusive evidence that verses 9-20 are not genuine. In fact, there is strong manuscript evidence in favor of their authority. However, the evidence is not conclusive enough either way to dogmatically assume a solution. Even if Mark 16:9-20 was not recorded by Mark, it does seem to be a genuine primitive addition. In such a case it would be just as real as Joshua's concluding summary of Moses' death in Deuteronomy 34:1-12.

Assuming the longer ending is authentic, let us make several observations.

1. Jesus was addressing the disciples and referring to those immediate converts who would believe the apostles' preaching (v. 20).
2. The singular purpose of the "signs" was to confirm the word preached (v. 20).
3. There is not the slightest hint that those phenomena (the signs) would be continued beyond the ministry of the apostles.
4. Either *all* the signs are present today or none of the signs is currently active. Nowhere in the church today do all or any of those signs authenticate a salvation experience in a new convert (v. 17) and thus confirm the truth of the word preached (v. 20).
5. The fulfillment of verses 17-18 was experienced by the apostles among their converts, as explained in verse 20.

Sufficient proof is lacking to substantiate any one of the three possible endings of Mark 16. However, our brief investigation of verses 9-20 indicates that if the longer option contains the true words of Christ, He limited its fulfillment to the time of the apostles and their immediate converts.

But we need to exercise caution. Because the textual evidence

2. Bruce M. Metzger, *A Textual Commentary on the Greek New Testament* (New York: United Bible Society, 1971), p. 126.

(not interpretation) is uncertain, it is best not to use Mark 16:9-20 as biblical support for any theological position. A. T. Robertson has wisely cautioned against a dogmatic use of those verses:

> The great doubt concerning the genuineness of these verses (fairly conclusive proof against them in my opinion) renders it unwise to take these verses as the foundation for doctrine or practices unless supported by other genuine portions of the N.T.[3]

JOHN 14:12

> Truly, truly, I say to you, he who believes in Me, the works that I do shall he do also; and greater works than these shall he do; because I go to the Father.

Christ addressed the eleven disciples (Judas had already departed) and told them that the disciples present, who were believing in Him, would do the same works as Christ (see Acts 2:22 and Hebrews 2:4) and greater works; that is, not only would they do sign miracles but also greater works through those sign miracles.

The earlier inductive study of Acts and the epistles revealed that the disciples did not do greater sign miracles than Christ either in quantity or quality. In fact, they were fewer in quantity. Also, they did not perform miracles of creation (bread, fish, wine) or miracles in nature (calming storms, maneuvering fish).

How do we know whether the believing ones of John 14:12 were the immediately present disciples or all believers? To answer that key question, note first that Christ was addressing only the eleven. We are faced with the dilemma of limiting the passage to the immediate hearers only or concluding that it is also true for all believers in the church age.

It seems obvious that Christ was addressing the disciples, because He used the personal pronoun *you* throughout the passage. It is unwarranted to assume that Christ switched from addressing the disciples in 14:10-11 to all believers in 14:12 and then reverted back to the disciples in 14:13. Just as we would not

3. A. T. Robertson, *Word Pictures in the Greek New Testament*, 6 vols. (Nashville: Broadman, 1930), 1:405.

understand Christ's commission to the twelve in Luke 9 to apply to all believers, neither is such an understanding demanded or even necessary in John 14:12.

Why would the disciples be able to do greater works? Christ explained, "I go to the Father." Now if those greater works were merely physical miracles, Christ would not need to go to the Father, because the Father was already doing them through Him on earth. Christ went to the Father to be our priestly intercessor before the throne of God (1 Timothy 2:5). The book of Hebrews explains Christ's work in the presence of the Father (Hebrews 1:3; 4:14-16; 7:23-28; 9:11-28). The greater works that the disciples would do were evidently associated with the spiritual miracle of salvation (John 3:1-21).

John 5:20-21 verifies that interpretation. Verse 20 refers to "works" and "greater works than these." Verse 21, parallel with verse 20, explains that the "works" were physical miracles (resurrection only to die physically again), and the greater works were spiritual miracles (eternal life).

Jesus told the seventy when they returned not to rejoice in physical miracles but rather in their own salvation: "Nevertheless do not rejoice in this, that the spirits are subject to you, but rejoice that your names are recorded in heaven" (Luke 10:20).

John 14:12 does not promise that Christians today will do the same physical miracles or greater physical miracles than Christ. However, it does teach that a single person won to the Lord Jesus Christ is greater than any physical miracle Christ ever did. There will be more joy in heaven over one sinner who repents than over ninety-nine righteous persons who need no repentance (Luke 15:7, 10).

1 CORINTHIANS 12:9, 28, 30

To another faith by the same Spirit, and to another gifts of healing by the one Spirit. . . . And God has appointed in the church, first apostles, second prophets, third teachers, then miracles, then gifts of healings, helps, administrations, various kinds of tongues. . . . All do not have gifts of healings, do they? All do not speak with tongues, do they? All do not interpret, do they?

Admittedly, "gifts of healings" is the most enigmatic phrase that deals with healing in the entire Bible! Why? Because that phrase is mentioned only three times in the New Testament and all three instances are in 1 Corinthians 12. There is no further explanation of what the manifestation involved. It does not appear in other New Testament gift lists. So there is very little biblical evidence to draw from.

However, there are several biblical observations that help. First, both words in the term are plural—"gifts of healings." The plural surely does not require that it will be manifest on more than one occasion by the same person, for that would mean "word of wisdom" in 12:8 was a one-time occurrence only.

The parallel plurals "effectings of miracles," "distinguishings of spirits," and "kinds of tongues" could very well indicate that the manifestation was temporary (one time only) and had to be renewed by God at His will. For instance, Paul healed multitudes (Acts 19:11-12) but he couldn't heal himself (Galatians 4:13), Epaphroditus (Philippians 2:25-30), or Trophimus (2 Timothy 4:20). That would also explain why Paul did not direct Timothy (1 Timothy 5:23) to a person with that gift. Someone who had exercised it on one occasion would have no reason to suspect that it would be manifested again. James 5 can be similarly explained. This early epistle (about A.D. 50) exhorted sick ones to call for the elders rather than for one who manifested "gifts of healings."

Other than their association with the apostles, the "gifts of healings" are rarely seen. Only Philip is mentioned specifically (Acts 8:6-7). Stephen (6:8) and Barnabas (14:3) might also have exercised this sign gift. That would explain why Barnabas, who had healed with Paul in Iconium (v. 3), could not heal Paul when he was nearly stoned to death in Lystra (vv. 19-20).

The "gifts of healings" seems to be a sign that was given to authenticate the apostles (Hebrews 2:4). Therefore, it is not surprising to discover its conspicuous absence from the gift list of Romans 12, which was written later than 1 Corinthians. Once the apostles were authenticated and the early church established, the apostolic signs gradually disappeared, for they had served their God-intended purpose.

Neither is it surprising to see the total absence of sign gifts from the pastoral epistles written by Paul to Timothy and Titus. If those gifts were to be perpetuated, certainly Paul would have mentioned it, especially since Timothy suffered from stomach problems and other frequent afflictions (1 Tim. 5:23).

If "gifts of healings" was to be understood as something other than a miraculous sign gift, one would expect to see it manifested in the life of Paul's numerous associates. But there is no hint of its appearance after A.D. 59. It must be recognized that an argument from silence alone is not conclusive. Nevertheless, it is a piece of evidence to be considered with the other indications mentioned above.

Most likely, "gifts of healings" was a temporary gift used by God to authenticate the apostles, evidenced sparingly apart from Peter and Paul, and bestowed on a one-time basis only, to be renewed by God's sovereign will.[4] Therefore, the "gifts of healings" in 1 Corinthians 12:9, 28, and 30 were not necessarily intended by God to be manifested today.

Finally, the temporary nature of the "gifts of healings" does not mean that God is not divinely healing at His will today. Because the sparse number of healings in the Old Testament and the innumerable healings of Christ were not dependent on the "gifts of healings," neither is divine healing today dependent on that sign gift.

HEBREWS 13:8

Jesus Christ is the same yesterday and today, yes and forever.

Those who look for promises of healing often turn to this truth. They reason that because God healed in the past and never changes, He also must heal in the same way today.

Several errors exist in that kind of thinking. Biblically, we know that God will not heal forever. One day sin will be conquered and sickness will no longer exist; God's healing will not be needed. Just as it is not true to say that if God healed in the past He must heal forever, so also it is not true to say that if He healed in the past He heals today.

Within its context this passage is speaking directly of God's unchanging nature, not the varying manifestation of His nature (Malachi 3:6; Hebrews 1:12). Ananias and Sapphira offended God's holiness by lying and thus evoked His righteous wrath and died (Acts 5:1-11). God's holiness and righteousness never

---

4. J. Sidlow Baxter reached essentially this same conclusion in *Divine Healing of the Body* (Grand Rapids: Zondervan, 1979), pp. 281-83.

change, but He does not always strike each liar dead as soon as the untrue words are spoken.

What about Paul's unique visit to the third heaven (2 Corinthians 12:1-10)? Although God is still omnipotent, Christians today should not expect a similar trip.

God's goodness supplied the Jews supernaturally with food and clothing during their forty-year wilderness sojourn (Exodus 16:1-21; Deuteronomy 29:5). Christians are not expecting that kind of supply today, but God's goodness is still the same and will be forever.

Finally, Hebrews 13:8 generalizes the specific Old Testament illustration used as a promise in 13:5-6—that God is forever present with believers. In Acts 12 James and Peter were depending on God for protection. We know that James was executed and Peter miraculously released. God's unchanging nature was manifested in two entirely different ways within similar situations.

Here is a modern-day parallel to James and Peter.

In the June 1980 issue of *Our Daily Bread,* I told how a Christian providentially escaped death. An unexpected delay in New York kept him from catching Flight 191 in Chicago, which crashed with all 254 aboard. That article brought this note from a reader: "I just had to let you know about one of God's great saints who ran to make Flight 191—and made it!" His name was Edward E. Elliott, beloved pastor of the Garden Grove Orthodox Presbyterian Church in California. His plane from Pennsylvania was late, and a friend who had accompanied him to Chicago said he last saw him "dashing forward" in the terminal to make his connection.[5]

Hebrews 13:8 was equally true for both men. But one died while the other was spared.

In conclusion, Hebrews 13:8 does not promise believers that God will necessarily heal them today as He healed others in the past.

---

5. Dennis J. DeHaan, "Running to Heaven," *Our Daily Bread* (Grand Rapids: Radio Bible Class), 4 September 1981.

✦ 7 ✦

Does God Heal Today?

The abbey father exclaims, "It's a miracle!"

We ask, "Why?"

Because Brother Dominic has just zoomed through five months of copying in five minutes by using the latest brand-name copier. But while the ad uses an effective Madison Avenue anachronism, it was not a miracle.

A popular song affirms belief in miracles because someone has "seen the lily push its way up through the stubborn sod." But is that really a miracle?

Admittedly, it is difficult to define a supernatural phenomenon originated and controlled by the infinite God. However, any good definition should be able to withstand the test of biblical comparison. It should adequately describe and explain biblical miracles.

Many definitions of miracles have been offered. Here are some examples.

Agnes Sanford, a popular writer, believes that God's will includes unlimited miracles. She writes:

This was almost as great a miracle as the miracle of frost. . . . It was almost as great a miracle as the miracle of day and night, of sunrise and sunset, caused by the never ceasing swing of the earth and the sun and the moon in a pattern of motion controlled and adjusted by cosmic forces beyond the ken of the astronomer.[1]

In answer to *Christianity Today*'s question, "What is your definition of a miracle?" Kathryn Kuhlman replied:

Well, what a miracle may mean to you may not mean the same thing to me. I remember a little boy who recognized me on Wilshire Boulevard in Los Angeles and proceeded to tell me how a miracle had once happened to him: he found a quarter when he needed money. To someone else it may be the healing of cancer. Sometimes the supernatural happens, contradicting all known scientific laws. I believe that every birth is a miracle. Do you understand what I mean?[2]

Ruth Montgomery, in her book *Born to Heal*, explains miracles this way: "There is no such thing as a miracle."[3] She goes on to explain that what seems to be a miracle is merely the result of the correct application of natural laws. A miracle to her is simply what one does not yet understand.

C. S. Lovett, founder of Personal Christianity, takes this approach:

Do we not look on the healings performed by Jesus as miracles? Sure we do. Why? Because we don't understand the LAWS behind them. Just as a transistor radio would be a miracle to Paul, so do the New Testament healings seem miraculous to us.[4]

However, Lovett does admit that while he feels many of the healings in the New Testament are easily explained by those laws, not all of them are.[5]

1. Agnes Sanford, *Healing Light* (Reprint ed., Plainfield, N.J.: Logos, 1972), p. 4.
2. Kathryn Kuhlman, "Healing in the Spirit," *Christianity Today*, 20 July 1973, p. 6.
3. Ruth Montgomery, *Born to Heal* (New York: Coward, McCann & Geoghegan, 1973), p. 17.
4. C. S. Lovett, *Jesus Wants You Well* (Baldwin Park, Calif.: Personal Christianity, 1973), p. 18.
5. Ibid., p. 13.

E. J. Carnell, former Fuller Theological Seminary professor, explains a miracle as "an extraordinary visible act of divine power, wrought by the efficient agency of the will of God, through secondary means, accompanied by valid, covenantal revelation, and having its final cause the vindication of the righteousness of the Triune God."[6]

According to Reformed theologian Loraine Boettner, a miracle may be defined as "an event in the external world, wrought by the immediate power of God, and designed to accredit a message or messenger."[7]

The vast differences in those definitions highlight the widespread confusion today concerning "miraculous healing" and other alleged miraculous phenomena. The term *miracle* is not always well defined and is sometimes used inappropriately.

A BIBLICAL DEFINITION

The Bible defines a miracle with various words describing the "rainbow effect" of a miracle.

THE OLD TESTAMENT

In the Old Testament, four different Hebrew words describe the various shades of a miracle.

1. *Pele'* has the basic idea of "wonder." Exodus 15:11 and Psalm 77:11 are good illustrations.
2. *'Ot* indicates a "sign" that establishes a certainty that was not previously present. Exodus 4:8-9, Numbers 14:22, and Deuteronomy 4:34 are illustrative.
3. *Gebudāh* means "strength" or "might." Psalms 145:4, 11-12 and 150:2 are good examples.
4. *Mopēt,* the basic meaning of which is "wonder," "sign," "portent." It is used frequently in conjunction with

6. E. J. Carnell, *Introduction to Christian Apologetics,* 4th ed. (Grand Rapids: Eerdmans, 1952), p. 249.
7. Loraine Boettner, "Christian Supernaturalism," *Studies in Theology* (Reprint ed., Nutley, N.J.: Presbyterian and Reformed, 1974), p. 51.

'ot, as in Deuteronomy 4:34; 6:22, and Nehemiah 9:10.

THE NEW TESTAMENT

In the New Testament are four corresponding Greek words.

1. *Teras* ("wonder") is the miracle that is startling or imposing. Its extraordinary character is obvious. It indicates the marvel or wonder the miracle excites. It does not occur alone in the New Testament and is the Greek counterpart to *mopet* and *pele'* (see Deuteronomy 4:34, Septuagint). Acts 2:22 of Christ and Hebrews 2:4 of the apostles are good illustrations.
2. *Semeion* ("sign") leads a person to something beyond the miracle. It is valuable not for what it is but rather what it points toward. It is the Greek counterpart of *'ot* (see Numbers 14:22, Septuagint).
3. *Dunamis* ("power" or "miracle") illustrates the power behind the act and points to a new and higher power. *Gebudah* is the Hebrew equivalent (see Psalm 144:4, Septuagint). Acts 8:13 and 19:11 illustrate this use.
4. *Ergon* ("work") is used by Jesus in the gospel to describe distinctive works that no one else did (see John 15:24).

Those various elements constitute a biblical miracle. By combining those descriptive parts, a miracle from God may be defined as:

An observable phenomenon delivered by God directly or through an authorized agent (*dunamis*), whose extraordinary character captures the immediate attention of the viewer (*teras*), points to something beyond the phenomenon (*semeion*), and is a distinctive work whose source can be attributed to no one else but God (*ergon*).

That's a heavy definition. Boiled down to its core meaning, a miracle is "God calling time-out on natural laws and personally reaching into life to rearrange people and their circumstances according to His will."

PURPOSE OF BIBLICAL MIRACLES

Three statements in the New Testament speak directly to the question of the use of miracles.

First, Acts 2:22 is Peter's inspired commentary on the purpose of Jesus' miracles. "Men of Israel, listen to these words: Jesus the Nazarene, a man attested to you by God with miracles and wonders and signs which God performed through Him in your midst, just as you yourself know." Christ's works were displayed for the purpose of certifying His claims to deity and messiahship. The miracles of our Lord did not *prove* His deity, just as the apostolic miracles did not prove their deity. Rather, the miracles attested undeniably (John 11:47-48) to the truth of His claim to be the God-Man (John 14:10).

Next, 2 Corinthians 12:12 is a direct statement by Paul concerning miracles in relationship to the apostles. He states emphatically that the marks (*semeia*) of an apostle were signs, wonders, and miracles. Those supernatural phenomena from God were used to authenticate the apostolic messenger and thus validate his message (Acts 2:43 and 5:12). Much the same method was used by God to authenticate the Old Testament prophet—by fulfilling the prophet's message and through miracles (see Deuteronomy 13:1-5 and 18:21-22). Miracles distinguished between the true and the false.

Third, the author of Hebrews argues for the greatness of salvation. One of his proofs is that it was authenticated by God through miracles. Hebrews 2:4 states that God bore witness through the apostles (v. 3) by miracles.

Those three clear passages teach that God's primary purpose for miracles was to authenticate His messengers.

Illustrations of that major purpose are abundant in the Old Testament. In Exodus 3 and 4, God finally convinced Moses that he should represent Him in Egypt. To every one of Moses' objections or questions, God responded with a supernatural sign that would authenticate Moses' commission. In Exodus 4:30-31 the signs were performed and the Jews believed. After one sign and three plagues the magicians of Pharaoh believed (8:18-19). After ten plagues and the Red Sea incident, Pharaoh believed (14:26-30) and the Jews' faith was rekindled (14:31).

After feeding Elijah with her last morsels, the widow of Zarephath saw her food supernaturally replenished (1 Kings

17:8-16). At the death of her son she doubted (vv. 17-18). When her son was supernaturally brought back to life, she believed (v. 24). Elijah had been attested as authentic by a miracle from God. On Mount Carmel, fire from heaven at the command of Elijah made believers of the people in the midst of rampant unbelief and gross idolatry (18:30-40).

Naaman was convinced of Elisha's credibility after being healed of leprosy (2 Kings 5:14-15). Nebuchadnezzar knew Daniel's reliability after he correctly rehearsed and interpreted the king's dream (Daniel 2:46). God used miracles to authenticate His messenger. The miracles were never used merely for display, frivolity, or to exalt the messenger.

AN OVERVIEW OF MIRACLES IN HISTORY

The miraculous and the allegedly miraculous have both been evident in history. The Bible contains the only reliable account of God's miracles. To be sure, not all of the miracles that God performed are recorded in the Scriptures. John wrote twice (John 20:30; 21:25) that not all that Jesus did was recorded. However, the Bible clearly discusses those periods of history when God performed miracles through human agents.

BIBLICAL HISTORY

It is necessary to distinguish between those miracles performed directly by God (e.g., the destruction of Sodom, Genesis 19) and those performed by God through human agents, such as Moses, Elijah, Paul, or Peter.

A review of biblical history reveals three major time periods during which God performed miracles through men. These periods are:

Moses and Joshua, 1450-1390 B.C.
Elijah and Elisha, 860-800 B.C.
Christ and His apostles, A.D. 26-60

But even in those periods miracles were not the norm for all of God's servants. Speaking of John the Baptist, our Lord said,

"I say to you, among those born of women, there is no one greater than John" (Luke 7:28). John writes of the Baptizer and records, "While John performed no sign, yet everything John said about this man [Christ] was true" (John 10:41), although later John's message was vindicated by Christ's miracles. It is obvious that the stature of a man of God was not necessarily built by sign miracles, but rather by the truthfulness of his message.

EXTRABIBLICAL HISTORY

Reports of miracles are not limited to biblical history or Christianity. In fact, if the mere number of alleged miracles indicated something of the authenticity of a religion, Christianity would be eclipsed.

The fact that alleged miracles happen outside the Christian faith should cause Christians to be wary of those who claim to do the miraculous. Mormons, Christian Scientists, most Eastern religions, and pagan spiritists all claim miracles. They even claim that they have been verified by competent witnesses.

The history of alleged miracles within the sphere of Christianity since A.D. 100 is abundant in the area of healing. Benjamin Warfield, noted Presbyterian theologian, observes:

> There is little or no evidence at all for miracle-working during the first fifty years of the post-Apostolic church; it is slight and unimportant for the next fifty years; it grows more abundant during the next century (the third); and it becomes abundant and precise only in the fourth century, to increase still further in the fifth and beyond. Thus, if the evidence is worth anything at all, instead of a regularly progressing decrease, there was a steadily growing increase of miracle-working from the beginning on.[8]

Do the character and quality of postapostolic miracles match those recorded in Scripture? Philip Schaff, the eminent church

8. B. B. Warfield, *Miracles* (Reprint ed., London: Banner of Truth, 1972), p. 10.

historian, believes miracles extended beyond the apostolic age. However, he offers these weighty considerations against the majority of those miracles.

- They are of a much lower moral tone and far exceed biblical miracles in outward pomp.
- They do not serve to confirm the Christian faith in general.
- The further they are removed from the apostolic age, the more numerous they are.
- The church fathers did not truthfully report all there was to know about the alleged miracles.
- The church fathers admitted there were extensive frauds.
- The Nicene miracles met with doubt and contradiction among contemporaries.
- The church fathers contradicted themselves by teaching that miracles no longer took place and then reporting the occurrence of actual miracles.[9]

Thus, we need to heed history's warning regardless of our stand on miracles. Satan will do all he can to mislead and deceive Christians along the dead-end path of alleged miracles (2 Corinthians 11:13-15). Those on that path will one day approach Jesus with claims of their miracles in His name. To them He will respond, "I never knew you; depart from Me" (Matthew 7:22-23).

Therefore, Warfield's analysis of alleged postapostolic miracles stands as a solemn reminder and warning for us to be careful when faced with reports of the miraculous through human agents.

The common solution of this inconsistent attitude towards miracles, that the ecclesiastical miracles were only recognized as differing in kind from those of the Scripture, while going a certain way, will hardly suffice for the purpose. Ecclesiastical miracles of every conceivable kind

9. Philip Schaff, *History of the Christian Church*, 8 vols. (Reprint ed., Grand Rapids: Associated Publishers & Authors, n.d.), 3:191-92.

were alleged. Every variety of miracle properly so-called Chrysostom declares have ceased. It is the contrast between miracles as such and wonders of grace that Gregory draws. No doubt we must recognize that these Fathers realized that the ecclesiastical miracles were of a lower order than those of the Scriptures. It looks very much as if, when they were not inflamed by enthusiasm, they did not really think them to be miracles at all.[10]

ARE MIRACLES FOR TODAY?

The ultimate question to be answered is whether biblical miracles through men ceased. A frequent answer to that question is that biblical miracles never ceased altogether but rather became fewer in number because of increasing sin in the world. A. B. Simpson, founder of the Christian and Missionary Alliance church, wrote:

It remained in the church for centuries, and only disappeared gradually in the growing worldliness, corruption, formalism and unbelief. . . . This blessed gospel of physical redemption is beginning to be restored to its ancient place, and the church is slowly learning to reclaim what she never should have lost.[11]

Emily Neal noted forty-five years later:

Miraculous healings reminiscent of the New Testament are occurring in churches of every denomination all over the United States. They are the results of a revival of one of the Church's oldest and most dynamic ministries—the healing of sick bodies as well as souls. This ministry of the early church, though never wholly lost, has been rediscovered today with thrilling results.[12]

Have miracles through men really continued beyond the apostolic age? It was demonstrated from Scripture that their

10. Warfield, p. 48.
11. A. B. Simpson, *Gospel of Healing* (Harrisburg, Pa.: Christian Publications, 1915), pp. 10-11.
12. E. G. Neal, *God Can Heal You Now* (Englewood Cliffs, N.J.: Prentice Hall, 1958), p. 3.

function was to authenticate the messenger of God and ultimately God's message. When Revelation was recorded by John, the canon of the New Testament and the total revelation of Scripture from God was complete. After A.D. 95 there was no reason for God to perform miracles through men to authenticate His message. The canon was closed.

Again Warfield comments:

> These gifts were not the possession of the primitive Christian as such; nor for that matter of the Apostolic church or the Apostolic Age for themselves; they were distinctively the authentication of the Apostles. They were part of the credentials of the Apostles as the authoritative agents of God in founding the church. Their function confined them to distinctively the Apostolic Church, and they necessarily passed away with it.[13]

Admittedly, there is no one clear biblical statement that speaks directly to the question; however, if we consult the whole counsel of God, there are answers. Here are some New Testament indicators that the age of miracles through men ceased with the apostolic age.

Acts 2:22, 2 Corinthians 12:12, and Hebrews 2:4 indicate that sign miracles were for the purpose of authenticating the messenger of God. With the completion of the canon, those signs are no longer needed.

Just as there were miracles of benefit, there were also miracles of judgment. No one today would want to claim that God is dealing with liars as He did with Ananias and Sapphira (Acts 5:1-11). Neither would any would-be healer claim that God is supernaturally inflicting grave physical maladies through human agency such as the blindness inflicted upon Elymas by Paul (Acts 13:4-12). Either both or neither are present. That neither miracles of benefit nor miracles of judgment are present is supported both biblically and historically.

Following the historical sequence of the apostles who speak about miraculous gifts, miracles diminish in scope as time progresses. See 1 Corinthians (A.D. 55), Romans (A.D. 51), and Acts 19:11-12 (A.D. 52), where extraordinary miracles were occurring. Later epistles indicate those phenomena were wan-

13. Warfield, p. 6.

ing. Paul did not heal Epaphroditus (Philippians 2:27, A.D. 60). Trophimus was left sick by Paul at Miletus (2 Timothy 4:20, A.D. 64). Paul prescribed wine for Timothy's stomach ailment (1 Timothy 5:23, A.D. 62-63) rather than recommending that Timothy submit himself to one who healed. Paul himself had severe health problems (Galatians 4:13 and 2 Corinthians 12:7) that he could not miraculously cure.

James, writing before A.D. 50, exhorts those who are seriously ill to call for the elders to anoint and pray rather than to call for one with the ability to heal.

In the seven letters to the seven churches (Revelation 2:1—3:22, A.D. 95) no mention is made of miraculous sign gifts.

Thus the Scriptures teach that miracles through human agents served a very specific purpose. That purpose focused on authenticating the prophets and apostles of God as certified messengers with a sure word from heaven. When the canon of Scripture closed with John's Revelation, there was no longer a divine reason for performing miracles through men, and such miracles ceased.

IMPORTANT REMINDERS

Before we close our discussion of miracles in general, we need to make these observations.

If anything can become a miracle at the viewer's discretion, there would be no miracles at all, because miracles would lose their distinctive character and unique God-intended purpose.

Miracles, according to the biblical definition, preclude the necessity of secondary means and are not limited by the laws of nature. They involve God's supernatural intervention. Jesus' miracles were never limited; they were never doubted; they were performed in public; they were abundant and instant. Anything that would claim the title *miracle* today should also possess those qualities.

Miracles do not automatically produce spirituality in those who view them. The Israelites emancipated from Egypt very quickly degenerated into idol worshipers (Exodus 32) though the marvelous miracles of God were fresh in their minds. Elijah was involved in spectacular miracles from God, and yet the believing remnant was so small (7,000) that Elijah thought he was fighting the battle alone (1 Kings 19). After Jesus fed the 5,000 and spoke of the miracle's significance, many of His disciples withdrew and would no longer walk with Him (John 6:66).

DOES GOD HEAL TODAY?

I was recently thumbing through Philip Yancey's best-seller, *Where Is God When It Hurts?* In the opening chapter he narrates the dilemma of John and Claudia Claxton. Claudia contracted Hodgkin's disease soon after her marriage and had been given only a 50 percent chance to live.

Many of Claudia's friends stopped by the hospital to encourage her. Here is an account of one such visit.

> Another lady had dropped by who had faithfully watched Oral Roberts, Kathryn Kuhlman, and "The 700 Club" over the years. She told Claudia that healing was the only escape. "Sickness is never God's will," she insisted. "The Bible says as much. The devil is at work, and God will wait until you can muster up enough faith to believe that you'll be healed. Remember, Claudia, faith can move mountains, and that includes Hodgkin's disease. Truly believe that you'll be healed and God will answer your prayers."[14]

Claudia tried to build her courage and muster up her faith. But she grew weary in the process and concluded that she could never have enough faith. Claudia struggled with the question we want to answer—Does God heal today?

A BRAIN TEASER

Here is a tantalizing question: Is there anything that God cannot do? Think about it! Jeremiah asserts of God, "Nothing is too difficult for Thee" (Jer. 32:17).

So, let's answer no. But what about these verses? Read Titus 1:2: "God cannot lie," or 2 Timothy 2:13: "He [God] cannot deny Himself."

14. Philip Yancey, *Where Is God When It Hurts?* (Grand Rapids: Zondervan, 1977), p. 13.

What about Genesis 9:11? God can't flood the earth again. And James 1:13? God cannot be tempted.

How can we resolve those apparent contradictions? The issue actually involves God's nature and will, *not* His infinite power.

God cannot lie because that would contradict His true nature. He cannot be tempted because that would contradict His infallible Word. He cannot deny Himself because that would contradict His eternal existence. He cannot flood the world because that would contradict His revealed Word.

CRUCIAL QUESTIONS

Our brain teaser points out that God cannot and will not act contrary to His divine nature or revealed will. In those areas He is self-limited.

At this point let's consider some questions.

- Can God heal?
- Can God heal miraculously?
- Can God heal miraculously through men?

The answer to all three of those questions is overwhelmingly *yes*, as we showed earlier in our survey of the Scriptures.

These next three questions are not so easily answered.

- Will God heal?
- Will God heal miraculously?
- Will God heal miraculously through men?

The answers to our inquiries do not involve God's potential but rather His revealed practice. Our answers will be found not in God's unlimited capacity to work but in His conformity to His own will.

GOD'S PERSPECTIVE ON THE PHYSICAL

We need to back up and consider God's view of the physical side of life. Three perspectives are essential if we are to form adequate answers to the above questions. When we see God's view of the physical from the vantage of the metaphysical, the moral, and the material, we will begin to understand why God has acted the way He has in history.

THE METAPHYSICAL DIMENSION

The metaphysical, or God's sovereign involvement in our physical being, is first. Note what these Scriptures teach.

And the Lord said to him, "Who has made man's mouth? Or who makes him dumb or deaf, or seeing or blind? Is it not I, the Lord?" [Exodus 4:11]

See now that I, I am He, and there is no god besides Me; it is I who put to death and give life. I have wounded, and it is I who heal; and there is no one who can deliver from My hand. [Deuteronomy 32:39]

The Lord kills and makes alive; He brings down to Sheol and raises up. The Lord makes poor and rich. [1 Samuel 2:6]

But he said to her, "You speak as one of the foolish women speaks. Shall we indeed accept good from God and not accept adversity?" In all this Job did not sin with his lips. [Job 2:10]

The One forming light and creating darkness, causing well-being and creating calamity; I am the Lord who does all these. [Isaiah 45:7]

Is it not from the mouth of the Most High that both good and ill go forth? [Lamentations 3:38]

What do those Scriptures teach? Clearly that God is ultimately the *first cause* of all life, all death, all sickness, and all health. He shoulders that responsibility.

Many doctors acknowledge that. In difficult cases we frequently hear of doctors saying, "I have done my best; now it is in God's hands."

As I have lectured on this topic over the last seven years, I have presented these simple but thought-provoking questions to my audiences.

- Have you ever been sick?
- Did you recover from your infirmity?
- Have you been divinely healed?

Don't ever let anyone rob you of your joy of knowing that God was involved in your physical being. If you have ever recovered from an illness, in a very real sense you have been "divinely healed."

THE MORAL DIMENSION

Sin resulted from the Fall of Adam and Eve (Genesis 3:1-19). It will continue until the curse is removed (Revelation 22:3).

> Then when lust has conceived, it gives birth to sin; and when sin is accomplished, it brings forth death. [James 1:15]

> Therefore, just as through one man sin entered into the world, and death through sin, and so death spread to all men, because all sinned. [Romans 5:12]

After the Fall, God expressed His love toward believers in Christ. By God's mercy we sinners did not receive the death we deserved. To satisfy God's justice, Christ took upon Himself the penalty for the world's sins. Through God's grace we received what we do not deserve—eternal life in Jesus Christ.

But God's love does not negate the consequences of sin—two of which are sickness and death. Thus sin is the moral cause for all sickness. As long as sin exists in the world, so will sickness.

THE MATERIAL DIMENSION

Do you have one or more of the following problems?

Baldness	Wrinkles
Dandruff	False Teeth
Nearsightedness	Fatigue
Sagging muscles	Gray hair

There are many more such as accidents, germs, and genetic defects. They are all common signs of sin's material effects on our bodies and evidence that sin has afflicted everyone. Because all have sinned, all will die.

> When they sin against Thee (for there is no man who does not sin) and Thou art angry with them and dost deliver them to an enemy, so that they take them away captive to a land far off or near. [2 Chronicles 6:36]

He has not dealt with us according to our sins, nor rewarded us according to our iniquities. [Psalm 103:10]

Indeed, there is not a righteous man on earth who continually does good and who never sins. [Ecclesiastes 7:20]

For all have sinned and fall short of the glory of God. [Romans 3:23]

And inasmuch as it is appointed for men to die once, and after this comes judgment. [Hebrews 9:27]

It is simply not true that God's will is for every Christian to be perfectly healthy. We saw earlier that saints were sick and that God even afflicts with illness and death.

Unless we see God as metaphysically sovereign and sin as the moral cause of sickness, we will not fully understand the decaying world around us. Thus, when God does heal it is because of His grace, not because of our goodness.

WHAT ABOUT TODAY?

Will God heal today? Yes, we know that He will because of His promise revealed in James 5:15: "And the prayer offered in faith will restore the one who is sick, and the Lord will raise him up, and if he has committed sins, they will be forgiven him."

Will God heal today miraculously? Yes, for that does not violate His nature or His will.

Will God heal today miraculously through men? No. Such an approach does not serve His purposes. Remember Acts 2:22 and Hebrews 2:1-4.

Did God allow Claudia Claxton to die in the midst of her misery? He could have but He didn't. Instead, He chose to make her the object of divine healing. After receiving a series of cobalt treatments, her cancer was in remission.[15] God healed providentially through medical technology.

CONCLUSION

The thrust of our study is not to determine whether God can or cannot heal. He can and does!

Our examination of the Scriptures has demonstrated that

15. Ibid., p. 15.

there is no biblical basis for a ministry of miraculous healing directly *through a human healer* today. That ceased with the apostolic age. Alleged contemporary faith-healing ministries fall embarrassingly short of the biblical pattern in time, scope, and intensity.

On the other hand, God does at times act in such a way that only His direct intervention is an adequate explanation for physical healing.

Healing by God's direct intervention is not always instantaneous or always complete. Our Lord's unmistakable touch is not brought about by any demand, gimmick, method, or plea from a would-be healer. It is God's response to the earnest prayer of a believer that heals a child of the King for our Lord's glory.

✦ 8 ✦

Are Reported Healings Real?

The April 1977 issue of the *National Courier*, a former tabloid for the charismatic movement, carried the story of a girl who had been apparently physically normal at birth. However, her parents soon noticed that she moved her legs in a strange way.

An orthopedic surgeon took X-rays and discovered that the ball of her left hip joint was out of its socket. Her parents later took her to a church where they requested an anointing service for the child.

After the service, the parents went back to the specialist for confirmation of the healing. X-rays were taken for a second time and showed that the ball was back in its socket. The doctor announced that there was no need for surgery. His concluding remark to the parents was, "I guess your religion works."[1]

Dr. Jerome Frank, professor of psychiatry at Johns Hopkins University, estimates that there are more patients treated by healers who are not licensed medical doctors than by those who

---

1. Harry Swofford, "Miracles," *National Courier*, 29 April 1977, p. 36.

are.[2] Those people reason that since their religion works, why should they go to an expensive professional?

We concluded earlier that God can do anything but that He works only within the framework of His nature and revealed will. We also determined that He is no longer healing through human healers. How then can we possibly account for all of today's reported healings? Are they *all* fraudulent or from Satan?

The following list of nine possible explanations may help to answer that important and practical question.

MISLEADING REPORTS

Oftentimes an alleged healing is supported by people because of a misleading report. That is, the sincerely given report just does not match the facts as they occurred. A vivid illustration of that was provided by George Peters, former professor of missions at Dallas Theological Seminary. Having heard many stories of healings from the Indonesian revival (written about by Mel Tari in *A Mighty Wind*), Peters decided to go to Indonesia to interview the people and find out firsthand what had happened.

He talked to people who were "raised from the dead" and questioned those who had been healed. His findings were published in the book *Indonesian Revival*. One portion of what he wrote deals with people who were raised from the dead. He reports:

> The reports from Timor that God raised some people from the dead have startled many American Christians. I do not doubt that God is able to raise the dead, but I seriously question that He did so in Timor. In fact, I am convinced that it did not happen. Let me explain:
>
> I visited a man who is known in the community as having been raised from the dead. I met a woman who reported that her infant daughter of four months had been raised. I talked to the woman who was said to be responsible for having brought back to life two people, and to the man who claimed to have been instrumental in raising two people

2. "Science Takes New Look at Faith Healing," *U.S. News & World Report*, 12 February 1979, p. 68.

from the dead, a boy of twelve and a man forty to forty-five years old.

In my questioning, I kept the sentiments of the people in mind. Their absolutist beliefs will not respond to questions of doubt. I was also aware of the fact that their word for death may mean unconsciousness, coma, or actual death. I also knew of their traditional belief in the journey of the soul after death from the body to the land of the ancestors.

I had to explore the experiences of these people while they were in the state of death, how far they had "traveled," so to speak, between death and resuscitation. It became apparent that death takes place in three stages, according to their beliefs. In the first stage, the soul is still in the body; in the second stage, the soul may be in the home or immediate community; and in the third stage, the soul takes its flight to the beyond and the land of the ancestors. Not one of the dead persons believed his soul had completely departed to the region beyond. That is the region of no return.

Those who claimed to have experienced resuscitation and immediate restoration were people who had died suddenly. Several children who had died after suffering prolonged illnesses had more gradual restorations.

I noted several interesting facts regarding the experiences reported during the state of death. One man told me that his soul had been so near his body during his state of death that he was able to hear people come near to his body. However, he was not able to speak or move. He was able to relate experiences during his state of death. After some questioning, his wife added, "My husband was not absolutely and totally dead." This led to some further probing and lengthy discussions. The mother whose infant daughter was raised was quite sure that her soul had not left her body, for she had been dead only about half an hour. An older man was able to describe his condition after dying. While dead he had promised God that if he could ever live again he would confess his sins and pay back the money that he had stolen from an evangelist. He was sure that this theft had caused his sudden death, and so was the evangelist who brought him back to life. Thus the stories went. Two younger boys, one four and another eight, were not able to recount their experiences while dead. However, they were sure that they had not yet left the earth.

I shall leave any judgments about these miracles to the reader. I went away satisfied that according to *their usage* of the word *death*, and their *concept* of death, they had experienced resuscitation. According to my concept of death, no such miracles happened; I learned again the value of seeing words and concepts from the people's point of view and interpreting them according to their mentality and understanding.[3]

Those people were in a state of unconsciousness or in a comatose state. They had not reached the point where their life processes were irreversibly stopped—from which point no human being can return unless God supernaturally intervenes.

Our first possible explanation for reported "healing" miracles is that the reports (however sincere the reporter) may not accurately portray what took place. What *seemed* to happen was not what *truly* happened.

DELIBERATE FRAUD

I hesitate to give the second reason because it may sound cynical, but I will document it. We need to admit there have been cases of deliberate fraud.

This example first appeared in the *National Courier*. Later, *Moody Monthly* published a follow-up report.

Last fall the *National Courier*, a biweekly tabloid published by Logos International, launched a testimonial series on miracles. One of the first stories was about faith healer Alice Pattico, who claimed she had been healed in a 1974 Kathryn Kuhlman meeting from breast and brain cancer and addiction to pain-killing drugs. She said her breasts, which had been removed in surgery, were restored, and that God had filled thirteen holes that had been drilled in her head in 1973 to administer laser beam surgery. She and her husband provided the *Courier* with doctors' letters to document her claims.[4]

In a later issue the *Courier* forthrightly took it all back.

SATANIC INVOLVEMENT

Is Satan ever involved in healing? Second Corinthians 11 indicates that Satan disguises himself and his "apostles" as angels of light. They appear and act as though they are from God. They come just as close to the real thing as they can while all the time being false.

3. George W. Peters, *Indonesian Revival* (Grand Rapids: Zondervan, 1973), pp. 80-83.
4. "Retraction," *Moody Monthly*, February 1977, p. 53.

For such men are false apostles, deceitful workers, disguising themselves as apostles of Christ. And no wonder, for even Satan disguises himself as an angel of light. Therefore it is not surprising if his servants also disguise themselves as servants of righteousness; whose end shall be according to their deeds. [2 Corinthians 11:13-15]

We do know that in Satan's attempts to imitate God he can hurt people. Job is the most familiar illustration. Remember also the lady that was afflicted for eighteen years, probably by Satan through demons. "And this woman, a daughter of Abraham as she is, whom Satan has bound for eighteen long years, should she not have been released from this bond on the Sabbath day?" (Luke 13:16).

Not only can Satan hurt, but he also has the potential to heal. Revelation 13:11-14 talks about Satan's working signs, wonders, and miracles—the same words used of our Lord and the apostles when they healed.

We do not honestly know whether or not Satan is healing today. The Bible gives no record of healing by Satan apart from Revelation 13. We can conclude this much: he definitely has the capacity to heal and he does imitate God. Healing miracles could serve his purpose.

HEALING CAPACITY OF THE BODY

This explanation is probably most often overlooked. Our bodies are incredible pieces of machinery. God created them with such marvelous design that they have the capacity to heal themselves of many physical problems.

Recently, someone shared this interesting article with me.

Is modern medical treatment more likely to kill than cure? Statistics gathered after "doctor strikes" indicate that today's physicians may not be living up to the first part of the Hippocratic oath, admonishing them to do no harm.

As a protest to soaring rates for malpractice insurance, doctors in Los Angeles went on strike in 1976. The result with no doctors around? An 18 percent drop in the death rate. That same year, according to Dr. Robert S. Mendelsohn, doctors in Bogota, Colombia, refused to provide any services except for emergency care. The result was a 35 percent drop in the death rate. When Israeli doctors drastically reduced their daily patient contact in 1973, the Jerusalem Burial Society reported that the death rate was cut in half. The only similar drop had been 20 years earlier at the time of the last doctors' strike.[5]

We have all suffered a superficial cut. The broken skin developed a scab and healed. We have recovered from colds, the flu, and numerous other physical problems without medical aid.

WRONG MEDICAL DIAGNOSIS

An illness sometimes is diagnosed wrongly. As a result, prescribed treatment for the mistaken illness is ineffective. The patient may then go to a healer who supposedly heals a diagnosed disease. Thus the healer is credited with healing the disease; but in reality the person never had the disease.

Under those circumstances, the conclusion is very misleading. The doctor is heralded as a brilliant diagnostician but a poor practitioner. The healer is billed as being superior to the medical profession.

PSYCHOGENIC ILLNESS

Doctors have confirmed that a psychogenic illness can falsely register an apparent physical infirmity in the mind. We normally call that a psychosomatic illness. Therefore, a change of mind can often cause a change in physical well-being.

William Nolan, a world-renowned surgeon, tells of an amazing case of pseudocyesis (false pregnancy) that he encountered as a young Army doctor. He treated a thirty-five year old woman who had been married twelve years and had all of the signs of pregnancy.

He followed the pregnancy for seven months and all appeared normal. But in her eighth month an associate discovered that the woman actually had a false pregnancy. After that, it took only a short while for her body to return to normal.[6]

EMOTIONALLY INDUCED ILLNESS

Doctors agree that stress can have a severely debilitating

5. Irving Wallace, David Wallechinsky, and Amy Wallace, "Doctors May Be Harmful," *Parade*, 4 October 1981, p. 27.

6. William A. Nolan, *Healing: A Doctor in Search of a Miracle* (Greenwich, Conn.: Fawcett, 1976), pp. 253-55.

effect on the body. Kenneth Pelletier wrote these significant words:

> Medical and psychological problems caused by stress have become the number one health problem in the last decade. One standard medical text estimates that 50 to 80 percent of all diseases have their origin in stress. Stress-induced disorders have long since replaced infectious disease as the most common maladies of people in the post-industrial nations.
>
> During recent years, four disorders—heart disease, cancer, arthritis, and respiratory diseases such as bronchitis—have become so prominent in the clinics of the United States, Western Europe and Japan, that they are known as "the afflictions of civilization." Their prevalence stems from poor diet, pollution, and most important, the increased stress of modern society.[7]

Emotionally induced illnesses frequently have a reversible process. Removing the stress also helps to remove the physical symptoms caused by that stress. Psalm 32 reveals that the cause of David's physical distress was guilt over his sin with Bathsheba.

When I kept silent about my sin, my body wasted away
Through my groaning all day long.
For day and night Thy hand was heavy upon me;
My vitality was drained away as with the fever heat of
    summer.
I acknowledged my sin to Thee,
And my iniquity I did not hide;
I said, "I will confess my transgressions to the
    Lord";
And Thou didst forgive the guilt of my sin.
Therefore, let everyone who is godly pray to Thee in a time
    when Thou mayest be found;
Surely in a flood of great waters they shall not reach him.
Thou art my hiding place; Thou dost preserve me from
    trouble;
Thou dost surround me with songs of deliverance.

Psalm 32:3-7

7. Kenneth Pelletier, "Mind as Healer, Mind as Slayer," *Christian Medical Society Journal* 11, no. 1 (1980): 8.

When David confessed his sin and regained peace of mind, he was restored to physical health. However, it is not always true that emotionally induced illnesses are reversible. For example, you may get rid of your stress but retain an ulcer.

THE DOCTOR'S TREATMENT WORKED

Most people who go to faith healers and claim to be healed have also been to doctors. They have had medicine, and some have even had operations. In spite of that, they do not think to give the doctor credit for their healing.

Jesus recognized the importance of doctors. He said that it is not those who are healthy who need a physician but those who are ill. He related the story of the good Samaritan, who used oil and wine as the basic medicines of the day. He chose a medical doctor (Luke the beloved physician) to be one of Paul's companions and to write two books in the New Testament.

Healers sometimes malign the medical profession. They use Mark 5:26 for their proof text. In that passage a certain woman spent all of her money on doctors, with no results. One day she touched Jesus' cloak as He passed; power went out from Him and she was healed. Mark was not being derogatory about medical practitioners of the day. He was just recognizing the fact that the woman had been to doctors but could not be cured. No conclusions are drawn. Nowhere does our Lord defame or denounce the medical profession.

GOD HEALED

That God can directly intervene and heal is a very legitimate possibility. However, it is wrong to say that God intervened miraculously through a human channel to heal. Biblically, there is nothing to prevent God's reaching down directly to restore one's health. To say anything less would be to limit God in ways that He does not limit Himself.

CONCLUSION

The next time you hear of a reported healing, don't jump to conclusions. Make sure you have all of the facts. Think through all of the possibilities and their various combinations outlined here.

You can be sure that there is no miraculous ministry of healing *through men* as there was through the prophets, Jesus, or the apostles. Those who attempt to heal in that way are presumptuous, as were the sons of Sceva (Acts 19:11-16) and Simon (8:9-24).

William Nolan set out several years ago to investigate faith healing. His findings and conclusions are recorded in *Healing: A Doctor in Search of a Miracle*. Here are Nolan's concluding thoughts, demonstrating that similar conclusions can be reached even though the subject of faith healing is approached from two different perspectives—medical and theological.

Two years ago I began looking for a healing miracle. When I started my search I hoped to find some evidence that someone, somewhere, had supernatural powers that he or she could employ to cure those patients we doctors, with all our knowledge and training, must still label "incurable." As I have said before, I have been unable to find any such miracle worker.

So, in a certain sense, I suppose, my two years have been wasted. Yet I hardly feel that's the case.

You see, looking into the healing phenomenon, becoming reacquainted with the interweaving and interdependency of the mind, the nervous system, and the body itself, I have become increasingly aware that all of healing is, in a very real sense of the word, miraculous. God has given us minds, the workings of which we have barely begun to comprehend, and using those minds, we have been able to find the answers to many of the puzzling disorders that afflict us. We have been able to extend our life span and raise the quality of our lives. Admittedly, we've created some new problems and haven't even begun to solve all the old. But we have made a start, and there's every reason to believe that if we persist, we will eventually find cures for many more of the diseases, physical and mental, that still afflict us.

What I've learned, and I hope I've been able to communicate something of this feeling, is that we don't need to seek out miracle workers if we're ill. To do so is, in a way, an insult to God.

Our minds and bodies are miracle enough.[8]

8. Nolan, p. 272.

Part Two

A Christian's Response
to Sickness

♦ 9 ♦

Faith, Prayer, and Doctors

One Monday morning I received a call from a woman who reported she had just tossed her prescriptions in the trash and claimed her healing by faith!

I congratulated that dear woman for wanting to place her faith in God and urged her to retrieve her medicine and to continue to follow the doctor's orders. Then I attempted to explain the right relationship between faith, prayer, and doctors.

My Monday morning caller was asking the questions that I want to deal with in the next few pages. Let's begin by asking what faith is.

WHAT IS FAITH?

We find faith's *definition* in Hebrews 11:1: "Now faith is the assurance of things hoped for, the conviction of things not seen." Augustine put it simply: "What is faith, unless it is to believe what you cannot see."

According to Romans 10:17 faith is *derived* from God's Word. It starts with Scripture, which has the capacity to generate faith in the redeemed listener.

Faith also has its *demand*—to believe that God is and to believe that God is a rewarder of those who seek Him (Hebrews 11:6). Without faith it is impossible to please God.

Paul highlights faith's *design* in 2 Corinthians 5:7: "For we walk by faith, not by sight." When the lights are out and the fog has rolled in, we are to navigate through life on instrument control. The Bible is our compass, and we are to follow it by faith wherever it guides.

Hebrews 4:2 presents the *dualism* of faith. The Word of God must not only be heard but also united with faith for it to be profitable.

The *duty* of faith is to live by it. "For in it the righteousness of God is revealed from faith to faith; as it is written, "But the righteous man shall live by faith" (Romans 1:17). Faith is to distinguish our lives.

Simply put, faith willingly takes the hand of God's Word and allows it to lead us through life—the dark and complicated or the simple and easy. Faith takes God at His Word and quietly obeys.

HOW IS FAITH MEASURED?

Is faith measured by the yard or meter? By the gallon or the liter? Though that might sound absurd, it is important to know how God measures faith.

When someone says, "Lord, give me more faith," how much are they asking for? How much faith is enough?

It is interesting that the Scriptures never give a unit of measurement for faith. Faith is merely described. That is illustrated in Matthew 8:10, where our Lord commends a man's faith: "Now when Jesus heard this, He marveled, and said to those who were following, 'Truly I say to you, I have not found such great faith with anyone in Israel.'" Jesus described the centurion's faith as "great." He had the same reaction to the Canaanite woman in Matthew 15:28: "O woman, your faith is great."

How then did Christ rebuke faithlessness? He most often responded, "O men of little faith" (Matthew 6:30; see also 8:26; 14:31; 16:8). In Matthew 17:19-20 the disciples had been unsuccessful in their attempt to exorcise a demon. So they asked Jesus the reason. He rebuked them for their "littleness of faith" and went on to say, "If you have faith as a mustard seed, . . . nothing will be impossible to you."

What did Christ mean? Simply this: it is not the size of faith (the mustard seed was the smallest garden variety seed, Matthew 13:32), but rather where and under what conditions the seed is planted.[1] If God is the sole object of our faith, then all things are possible to the believer because all things are possible for the One in whom faith's seed is planted (Matthew 17:20; Mark 9:23; Luke 18:27). God's will is the controlling factor of what He will do for us and through us.

The only requirements for our faith are that it not depend on sight (2 Corinthians 5:7), that it be without doubting (James 1:5-8), that it believes God can do all things (Matthew 19:26), and that it be satisfied to let God's will prevail (1 John 5:14).

On occasion, personal faith was not a necessary requirement for healing. It is obvious that Lazarus, Jairus's daughter, and the widow's son were incapable of displaying faith, yet, they were raised from the dead.

At times Christ healed when faith was displayed by someone other than the afflicted one. Those who claim that a person is unhealed due to his own lack of faith have missed God's mark of truth.

Occasionally the faith of the afflicted was commended, but almost never was it a prominent or necessary feature of Christ's healing ministry.

The book of Acts and the epistles both correspond to the gospels' record that faith was not required for healing. Note James 5:15, where the faith of the elders is demanded, not the faith of the afflicted.

At times, the faith of the afflicted was commended as in the gospels (Acts 3:16; 14:8-10). More often a personal faith was not required of the afflicted. Also, faith is not mentioned as a requirement for healing in the Old Testament. Naaman, the reluctant Syrian, is a classic example (2 Kings 5:1-14).

Now, consider this related question. How much faith is required for one to be saved? If the sick person will exercise the faith he had for salvation and trust God to work according to His will regardless of the outcome, then he will be a person of faith.

1. John Sproule, "The Problem of the Mustard Seed," *Grace Theological Journal* 1, no. 1 (Spring 1980): 37-42.

The answer is that it is not the amount of faith but the Person in whom that faith is placed that is important. Nowhere in the Scriptures is anyone admonished to measure his faith. That would be impossible. A person either believes or he does not believe. There is no middle road.

Prayer is the natural response of faith in our heavenly Father. So we need to turn our attention to prayer.

THE PROCESS OF PRAYER

Prayer follows a basic pattern.[2] First there is *admission*—"I can't do it myself."

> Abide in Me, and I in you. As the branch cannot bear fruit of itself, unless it abides in the vine, so neither can you, unless you abide in Me. I am the vine, you are the branches; he who abides in Me, and I in him, he bears much fruit; for apart from Me you can do nothing. [John 15:4-5]

The beginning step of fruitful prayer is always to acknowledge that apart from Jesus Christ we are, in God's mind, helpless creatures. The sooner we acknowledge that humbling truth, the sooner we will know God's intentions for us.

Next comes *submission*. We are to bow our desires before the presence of our sovereign Savior.

When Jesus taught the disciples to pray, He said, "Thy will be done, on earth as it is in heaven" (Matthew 6:10). When He agonized in Gethsemane's garden, His last words were, "Yet not as I will, but as Thou wilt" (Matthew 26:39). Thus our prayers should be like the Savior's—"Lord, let my will always be brought into submission with Yours." That leads to the third stage— *transmission*. Jesus modeled the pattern when He prayed, "Our Father who art in heaven" (Matthew 6:9). Because we do not know how to pray, God's Spirit intercepts our petition and intercedes on our behalf (Romans 8:26). We can confidently know that He is able to do exceeding abundantly beyond our request (Ephesians 3:20).

Meditate on that aspect of God's nature. We can pray as high

2. I am indebted to Dr. James L. Boyer, professor emeritus of Greek and New Testament at Grace Theological Seminary, Winona Lake, Indiana, for this insightful outline.

or as far as our human capacities allow us, and still we will not have begun to equal the mind of God. That's our heavenly hope when we send our deepest needs before the gracious throne of our heavenly Father (Hebrews 4:16).

The fourth step might just be the hardest—waiting on God. The *intermission* period from the time we ask until the time God answers can sometimes seem like forever. We sometimes want to scream out, "Lord, please hurry—I can't wait any longer."

Jesus anticipated our need and gave us an instructive parable about a nasty judge and a needy widow (Luke 18:1-8). The purpose of the parable is to show that we ought always to pray and not to lose heart if the answer is not immediately forthcoming.

Finally comes God's response. I believe God always answers prayer. He does it either through *permission* or *revision*, that is, He says either yes or "another way!"

At times He *delivers* as we pray. For example, Peter miraculously escaped from his Roman guards while the Jerusalem church prayed (Acts 12:5-17). At times God *detours*, such as He did with Christ. Instead of allowing Christ to ascend before Calvary, that ascension did not occur until afterward (Mark 14:36). He reached His destination but by an alternative route.

God also *delays*. Zacharias and Elizabeth had prayed for a son over the decades of their married life. It was not until they were beyond childbearing age that God answered (Luke 1:13).

God also can say no.

> If I regard wickedness in my heart, the Lord will not hear." [Psalm 66:18]

> So when you spread out your hands in prayer, I will hide My eyes from you, yes, even though you multiply prayers, I will not listen. Your hands are covered with blood. [Isaiah 1:15]

That ought not to be surprising, for Scripture tells us that "we do not know how to pray as we should" (Romans 8:26). God knows what is best even if He responds negatively. So do not be discouraged or give up on God when the answer is no.

The next time you pray for healing (or anything else, for that matter), rehearse those biblically outlined steps and make sure that you willingly and obediently follow them.

KEYS TO FRUITFUL PRAYER

Someone has remarked, "When you get caught on water in the middle of a raging storm, row for shore as though your safety depended on you while praying as though it all depended on God." The point of the story is this: life always involves the unexplainable combination of God's sovereignty and man's responsibility. Of the two, God will always be the determining factor.

The same is true of prayer. God knows our needs ahead of time (Matthew 6:8). He is able to provide exceeding abundantly beyond anything we can ask or think (Ephesians 3:20). But Christians are still commanded by Scripture to pray, and that without ceasing (see 1 Thessalonians 5:17).

These next thoughts on prayer relate specifically to our human responsibility as given by God. They focus primarily on who we are in the sight of God based on what we do in the presence of men. Check yourself and see if you are praying as God instructed.

1. Praying for the right reasons

What is the source of quarrels and conflicts among you? Is not the source your pleasures that wage war in your members? You lust and do not have; so you commit murder. And you are envious and cannot obtain; so you fight and quarrel. You do not have because you do not ask. You ask and do not receive, because you ask with wrong motives, so that you may spend it on your pleasures. [James 4:1-3]

2. Praying in the right relationships

You husbands likewise, live with your wives in an understanding way, as with a weaker vessel, since she is a woman; and grant her honor as a fellow heir of the grace of life, so that your prayers may not be hindered. [1 Peter 3:7]

3. Praying with the right rest

But if any of you lacks wisdom, let him ask of God, who gives to all men generously and without reproach, and it will be given to him. But let him ask in faith without any doubting, for the one who doubts is like the surf of the sea driven and tossed by the wind. For let not that man expect that he will receive anything from the Lord, being a double-minded man, unstable in all his ways. [James 1:5-8]

4. Praying with the right responses

And whatever we ask we receive from Him, because we keep His commandments and do the things that are pleasing in His sight. [1 John 3:22]

5. Praying in the right realm

And this is the confidence which we have before Him, that, if we ask anything according to His will, He hears us. And if we know that He hears us in whatever we ask, we know that we have the requests which we have asked from Him. [1 John 5:14-15]

6. Praying with the right restraint

Now He was telling them a parable to show that at all times they ought to pray and not to lose heart. [Luke 18:1]

When we meet all of those conditions we are delighting ourselves in God. If we do that, He promises then to give us the desire of our heart (Psalm 37:4).

But what if God does not answer immediately or in the way we prayed? It may simply mean that God's delay is not necessarily God's denial. Or it can mean that we have prayed outside of God's will, and He has sovereignly prevailed in the circumstances. But be assured, whatever God does is always right (Psalms 19:8; 119:128).

DOCTORS AND MEDICINE

Many claim that the medical profession and medicine are a contradiction to prayer and faith for a Christian. That was the mistaken notion of the woman who phoned me that Monday morning.

John R. Rice made this keen observation.

> God can save a sinner without the use of any human aid, but certainly He does not usually do so. If God can use a man, with his consecrated wisdom and love and skill in winning a soul, why should He not use a doctor, a pharmacist, or a nurse with their consecrated skill in healing the sick?[3]

Asa (2 Chronicles 16:11-14) was not rebuked for merely going to a doctor, but because he disobeyed God by seeking a godless pagan physician rather than the divinely appointed Levitical priest (Leviticus 13).

Paul told Timothy to take wine (1 Timothy 5:23). He also traveled extensively with Luke, the beloved physician (Colossians 4:14). Jesus recognized doctors and medicine as legitimate agents (Matthew 9:12; Luke 10:25-37). In fact, there is not one verse of Scripture that hints that believers are not to use doctors and medicine.

The strongest biblical evidence that God intended believers to use medical means is the health aspects of the Mosaic legislation. Consider these laws:

- sanitation (Exodus 29:14; Deuteronomy 23:12-14)
- sterilization (Leviticus 11:32, 39-40; Numbers 19:11; 31:22-23)
- quarantine (Leviticus 13:1—14:57; Numbers 5:4)
- hygiene and diet (Leviticus 11:1-47)

Of those who condemn medicine, who would fail to wash with soap, stop brushing his teeth, stop eating, or stop exercising? All of those are essential to good health.

Loraine Boettner observes:

> We have no more reason to believe that our sicknesses and diseases will be cured without means than we have to believe that if we fail to plow and plant we will nevertheless be given food. . . . Surely faith-feeding

3. John R. Rice, *Healing in Answer to Prayer* (Murfreesboro, Tenn.: Sword of the Lord Publishers, 1944), p. 20.

is quite as rational as faith-healing. And if diseases are to be cured by faith, then why may not death, which is simply the result of disease or injury, also be eliminated in the same way?[4]

Medical practitioners are participants in the inexhaustible study of God's created processes. They are making God's creative genius available for the physical healing of the human race. Hospitals, the latest in medical technology, and sophisticated pharmaceuticals are all part of God's provision to restore a sick person to health.

However, where doctors and medicine can no longer help, faith and prayer continue. When we are sick, we must let the doctors work as though our health depended totally on them, while at the same time praying with faith as though our recovery rested totally in the sovereign hands of God.

If anyone ever tells you that you were not healed because your faith was insufficient, take heart in this realistic approach by J. I. Packer.

To be told that longed-for healing was denied you because of some defect in your faith when you had labored and strained every way you knew to devote yourself to God and to "believe for blessing," is to be pitchforked into distress, despair, and a sense of abandonment by God. That is as bitter a feeling as any this side of hell—particularly if, like most invalids, your sensitivity is already up and your spirits down.[5]

4. Loraine Boettner, "Christian Supernaturalism," *Studies in Theology* (Phillipsburg, N.J.: Presbyterian and Reformed, 1976), pp. 74-75.
5. James I. Packer, "Poor Health May Be the Best Remedy," *Christianity Today*, 21 May 1982, p. 15.

✦ 10 ✦

Are Anointing Services for Me?

"The Sacrament of the anointing of the sick is administered to those who are dangerously ill, by anointing them on the forehead and hands with olive oil, or if opportune, with another properly blessed vegetable oil."[1]

That statement is contained in a pamphlet entitled *Anointing and Pastoral Care of the Sick*. Its dateline is Rome, December 7, 1972, and its author is Pope Paul VI.

It was a radical change for the Roman church. For centuries they had used James 5 to support the sacrament of Extreme Unction, or Last Rites. It supposedly provided the forgiveness or removal of sin as a preparation for death.

The major change was in the omission of any mention of the danger of death as a condition of the anointing. The Roman church recognized that the context of James 5 depicts the experience of a Christian who is seriously ill but by no means just one breath from death.

Let's examine the text of James 5:14-20.

1. *Anointing and Pastoral Care of the Sick* (Washington: U.S. Catholic Conference, 1973), p. 5.

Is anyone among you sick? Let him call for the elders of the church, and let them pray over him, anointing him with oil in the name of the Lord; and the prayer offered in faith will restore the one who is sick, and the Lord will raise him up, and if he has committed sins, they will be forgiven him. Therefore, confess your sins to one another, and pray for one another, so that you may be healed. The effective prayer of a righteous man can accomplish much. Elijah was a man with a nature like ours, and he prayed earnestly that it might not rain; and it did not rain on the earth for three years and six months. And he prayed again, and the sky poured rain, and the earth produced its fruit. My brethren, if any among you strays from the truth, and one turns him back, let him know that he who turns a sinner from the error of his way will save his soul from death, and will cover a multitude of sins.

THE SITUATION
(James 5:14a)

James says in 5:13, "Is any among you suffering? Let him pray. Is any among you cheerful? Let him sing praises." The word for "suffering" in verse 13 is not to be confused with the word used for "sick" in verse 14 (although sickness could be a part of the suffering). The word *suffering* is a general word that may involve either mental or emotional suffering or a combination of both. James says that if you have a problem in your life because of suffering, you are to look to God and pray. If everything is going well and we are cheerful, we are to look to God with praise.

The word for "sick" in verse 14 is the Greek word *asthenia* and has the basic meaning of being weak either spiritually or physically. Only the context can give us the author's intended meaning, which we will see is not spiritual but physical. The important thing here is that the word means "to be weak." However, the term does not indicate the severity of the weakness.

Now look at verse 15. "The prayer offered in faith will restore the one who is *sick*" (italics added). The word *sick* is not the same Greek word as that used in verse 14—*asthenia* is used in verse 14 and *kamno* is used in verse 15. It is the parallel use of those two words that indicates the nature and severity of the weakness in the physical realm.

Kamno in its general sense means "fatigue," or something that is worn out or weary. It was used to describe documents that were worn out by frequent use.

In the physical realm the word means "hopelessly sick"; that is, sick to the point that death was imminent. Frequently it described those who were dead. Thus, we can begin to see why the Roman church used that passage to describe someone who was seriously ill. However, they interpreted wrongly. It wasn't to prepare someone for death; it was to restore someone to his former physical well-being.

The word *kamno* gives us an added dimension to help us understand that James is talking about a very serious physical illness.

THE SOLUTION

(James 5:14*b*)

If anyone is sick (physically sick in a severe way) "let him call for the elders." For someone with a severe infirmity that forbids mobility, it is understandable why James would recommend that that person call for the elders of the church instead of attempting to go to them. Therefore, anointing services that are held in the front of the church—the kind to which people can walk—are foreign to the language and meaning of James 5.

James was writing to Christians, regardless of their former religious heritage or nationality. This first of the New Testament documents was penned about A.D. 50.

James frequently uses a common New Testament term for Christians—*brethren*. He not only refers to them as brethren, but also writes of their personal faith in Jesus Christ. "My brethren, do not hold your faith in our glorious Lord Jesus Christ with an attitude of personal favoritism" (2:1). He is clearly stating that they had placed their faith in Jesus Christ.

He also implies that they were Christians in James 2:7: "Do they not blaspheme the fair name by which you have been called?" That name is *Christian,* which was first used in Acts 11:26.

The only people to whom the coming of the Lord is a hope are those who believe that Christ will fulfill His promises of redeeming and resurrecting them for eternity (see James 5:7-8). In Christ's church there has never been an authorized distinction between Jew and Gentile (Gal. 3:28). Therefore, the book of James was written for Christians, Jew or Gentile.

Who are the elders? They were the men whom God appointed to oversee the church. The qualifications for eldership are found in 1 Timothy 3:1-7 and in Titus 1:6-9. Three words in the New Testament describe the office, with each describing a different aspect of it. *Overseer* refers to the basic function; the idea of *elder* indicates the quality of one's life; and *pastor* implies the role of daily activities.

The sick Christian is to call for the elders. When the elders visit the person, they will be involved in three basic tasks. They will *pray* over him while *anointing* him with oil in the name of the Lord. Also, James 5:16 speaks directly of *confessing* sin to one another.

Consider the confession of sin. I have inferred from James 5:15-16 that unconfessed sin in the life of a believer is very possibly responsible for the weakened condition. Although sickness is not always a direct chastisement by God for sin in our lives, there were times in the Old Testament when God used affliction as a rod of chastisement.

If sin is the problem, then sickness can follow in the form of guilt over a sin (e.g., as David in Psalm 32) or directly from the sin itself. In 1 Corinthians 11 Paul said some of the Corinthians were sick and some of them even slept (were dead) because they made an abomination of the bread and the cup. James is emphasizing that spiritual matters have a priority over the physical. Confession of sin precedes the anointing with oil.

The question has often been raised as to whether the anointing is medicinal or symbolic. It is true that in the first century oil was used in a medicinal sense, and it was believed by the ancients that oil had a healing effect on people. The Samaritan picked up the man who had been mugged and robbed and rubbed oil and wine on his wounds (Luke 10:34). Mark 6:13 says that the apostles anointed people and healed them.

The normal word for symbolic anointing is not used here. The word in our text is normally used in extrabiblical Greek literature of anointing with oil for medicinal purposes. But three times in the Old Testament (the Septuagint translation— Genesis 31:13; Exodus 40:13; and Numbers 3:3) the Greek verb used in James 5:14 was used to translate the Hebrew word where symbolic anointing was in mind. Therefore, whether anointing is used in a medicinal or symbolic sense must be determined by the context.

But how does oil help cancer, tuberculosis, arteriosclerosis, or broken bones? Actually, it has no medicinal effect for any of those problems. Thus, we can suspect that the oil is used in a symbolic sense.

"Let them pray over him" (James 5:14). Who does the praying? The elders pray. A "prayer offered in faith will restore the one who is sick" (v. 15). So whose prayer and whose faith is it? It is the elders' prayer and faith; the faith of the sick person actually has nothing to do with it. He has already expressed his faith by calling the elders. That does away with the error that says if one has enough faith he will be healed, or that if a person is not healed at a healing service it was because of his lack of faith. Those common assertions do not square with the Scriptures.

THE RESOLUTION
(James 5:15)

"The prayer offered in faith will restore the one who is sick, and the Lord will raise him up, and if he has committed sins, they will be forgiven him."

Note that the instrument for raising up the sick person is not his prayer but that of the elders. The power that raises him up is not the elders' power or his faith; it is the Lord's direct intervention. Healing through the channel of human healers is absolutely foreign to this text.

"If he has committed sins" is a complex clause. It carries the idea of persistence. If someone has openly, knowingly, recklessly, and rebelliously persisted in sin, those sins will be forgiven him, which implies the sins have been confessed and forgiveness of sin has been asked of the Father.

The last clause in verse 15 is "they will be forgiven him." The Greek text actually says "*it* will be forgiven him." That is, not individual sins but the state of sin will be forgiven. It concerns a believer who has recklessly involved himself in sin without repentance. Perhaps such a person has succumbed to dishonesty or some other sin in his life.

These last two clauses of verse 15 give the condition that helps us understand its promise. The condition gives us the limitation of the passage. J. B. Mayor, who has written the most scholarly and complete commentary on the book of James, suggests that this passage ought to read: "If he has committed sins, which have given rise to the sickness."[2] The point of the passage then is this: a believer has wandered off into sin, remained in sin, and God has chastised him by bringing sickness into his life to bring him back to Himself. When the believer recognizes that God has brought a very untimely and severe illness to incapacitate him, he is to call for the elders of the church. The elders are to come; he is to confess sin; and they are to anoint him with oil and pray over him. If sin is the cause of sickness, then God will raise him up. If sin is cared for through confession, there will be no further need for chastisement. God takes away the chastisement and the believer is restored to physical health.

THE CONCLUSION
(James 5:16)

Confessing our sins to one another indicates that we are not living a reckless, abandoned life of sin. We are recognizing the sin in our lives, repenting of that sin before God, and asking one another's forgiveness for the sins we have committed. By so doing we will never reach the place where God has to chastise us with sickness. That is the thrust of this verse—confess your sins one to another and then pray for one another that you may be healed.

The Greek word used for "healed" can be used in a spiritual or physical sense. The idea of this verse suggests that James is talking about the spiritual sense.

THE ILLUSTRATION
(James 5:17-18)

Elijah was a man with a nature like ours, and he prayed earnestly that it might not rain; and it did not rain on the earth for three years and six months. And he prayed again, and the sky poured rain, and the earth produced its fruit. [James 5:17-18]

Elijah was a man with a nature like ours; a sinner who was redeemed by God's saving grace (see 1 Kings 17-18). In 1 Kings 17:1 Elijah prayed before the Lord. James 5:18 adds: "He

2. J. B. Mayor, *The Epistle of St. James* (Reprint ed., Grand Rapids: Baker, 1978), p. 168.

prayed again, and the sky poured rain, and the earth produced its fruit" (see 1 Kings 18:41-46).

What is the parallel idea? Israel sinned and God chastised her by withholding rain for three-and-a-half years. Elijah prayed (5:18). Why? In 1 Kings 18 we find the great confrontation between the prophets of Baal and Elijah on Mount Carmel. The prophets danced around, prostrated themselves, and shouted to Baal to call fire down from heaven and burn up the altar. Although they danced and shouted, nothing happened. Then Elijah completely doused his altar with barrels of water so that he could not be accused of faking fire. He prayed a short prayer and fire came down from heaven and devoured the altar so that there was nothing left but ashes. The people repented of their sin and killed the 450 prophets of Baal. God then told Elijah to pray for rain.

God had brought physical chastisement to the land because of the sins of the people. When the people repented before God, He restored that which He had withheld.

Elijah was characterized by his righteous lifestyle, which is the very same lifestyle that must characterize an elder in the church. A sinful population called Elijah, confessed their sin, and God then healed their land through Elijah's prayer for rain. The same is true in the physical realm according to James.

THE APPLICATION
(James 5:19-20)

My brethren, if any among you strays from the truth, and one turns him back, let him know that he who turns a sinner from the error of his way will save his soul from death, and will cover a multitude of sins.

The text could be amplified to read:

My brethren. if any believer among you strays from the truth and another believer turns him back so that he gets back on the straight and narrow, let him know that he who turns a sinner [a sinning Christian] from the error of his way, will save his soul from death.

Does not the saved person already have his soul redeemed? Once again the Greek helps us. The text here literally reads "will save a soul." The word for *soul* is frequently used to describe the person—the whole human being. The NIV translation catches James's thrust, "will save him from death."

The redeemed sinner will be saved from death, namely physical death, which can come through God's chastising discipline.

Thus, there are at least three conclusions we can draw from 5:19-20.

1. Believers are responsible for restoring straying brothers and sisters in the faith.
2. To continue in unchecked sin can result in death because the believer has disqualified himself from representing God or accomplishing His work.
3. Restoration is possible even if the sins are frequent and serious; confrontation will cover a multitude of sins. We cannot sin so badly that God cannot forgive us, but for God to forgive us, we need to turn from our sin back to God.

SUMMING IT UP

Because this is an important chapter, we need to capsulize our observations.

1. The sickness involved demands that the person be severely ill.
2. The sick person is necessarily a Christian.
3. The sick person is to call for the elders.
4. The elders are appointed leaders of the local congregation, who respond by coming to the afflicted.
5. After a time of confession of sin, the elders symbolically anoint the afflicted one and pray over him.
6. It is the Lord who raises up the afflicted.
7. If sickness is because of sin, and proper confession is made after the counsel of the elders, in faith we may expect healing according to God's Word. If sin is not the cause, simply pray the desires of your heart, leaving what is best for the individual up to God.
8. James 5:14-15 does not forbid or preclude the use of doctors or medicine.
9. Under those conditions, James 5:14-20 is applicable for today.

✦ 11 ✦

On My Back by Divine Design

"I just could not serve a God whose will it was not to heal everybody," a stewardess once responded to a conversation about divine healing. She manifested a very common response to sickness—that it is not God's will to allow sickness.

Another frequent reaction to suffering is that it must be caused by personal sin. In 1 Kings 17:18, when the widow's son died, she turned to Elijah and shrieked, "You have come to me to bring my iniquity to remembrance, and to put my son to death!" Elijah defused her verbal bomb by raising the young boy from the dead.

Does God ever use sickness for good? Is sickness caused only by personal sin? Can I be in the will of God and still be sick? Those are the questions that need to be answered from Scripture; here is a survey of what sickness can accomplish in the will of God.

EMPHASIZES GOD'S DIVINE NATURE

Unquestionably, Job suffered. The pressure was on from all sides. He had lost his family and belongings; only his wife survived and she told him to curse God. Finally, he was afflicted with a skin disease that defies our imagination. After all that happened, Job's friends engaged him in a theological debate over the whys of all those events.

When God could no longer tolerate their rambling discussions, He revealed Himself out of a whirlwind (Job 38-41). After it was over Job exclaimed: "I have heard of Thee by the hearing of the ear; but now my eye sees Thee; therefore I retract, and I repent in dust and ashes" (Job 42:5-6).

Job's calamity provided an opportunity for God to emphasize His divine reality in ways that otherwise would not have been needed. It is not uncommon for those who spend their days looking heavenward to find that the Lord shows Himself in special ways that only the circumstances of sickness and suffering make possible.

GLORIFIES GOD

One of Jesus' best friends was seriously ill. Lazarus's sisters sent for Christ with the message that the one whom Jesus loved was sick. Christ's initial response is insightful. He said, "This sickness is not unto death, but for the glory of God, that the Son of God may be glorified by it" (John 11:4).

If Lazarus had been healthy, the glory of God could not have been manifested through him by a supernatural restoration. Those who suffer are candidates to be vessels through whom Jesus Christ might be glorified.

DISPLAYS GOD'S WORK

One of Christ's most familiar healings is found in John 9:1-41. When confronted with a man who had been blind since birth, the disciples asked: "Rabbi, who sinned, this man or his parents, that he should be born blind?" (v. 2). Jesus responded, "It was neither that this man sinned, nor his parents; but it was in order that the works of God might be displayed in him" (v. 3).

After Jesus gave sight to the man, the work of God was displayed in him everywhere he went. His testimony was dynamic: "Since the beginning of time it has never been heard that anyone opened the eyes of a person born blind. If this man were not from God, He could do nothing" (vv. 32-33).

BRINGS MATURITY

How would you like to be mature, whole, and lacking nothing? Most Christians would respond with an overwhelming yes.

It's a great prospect, but it is the result of a process that James tells us about.

> Consider it all joy, my brethren, when you encounter various trials, knowing that the testing of your faith produces endurance. And let endurance have its perfect result, that you may be perfect and complete, lacking in nothing. [James 1:2-4]

Trials that test our faith produce patience. Patience when exercised leads to the wholeness that we all desire. Sickness and suffering are only some of the many trials that God uses in that process.

PREVENTS SELF-EXALTATION

Paul had been privileged to hear inexpressible words spoken in the third heaven. Because of the surpassing greatness of that experience, God allowed Satan to buffet Paul with a thorn in the flesh. Its purpose was to keep Paul from exalting himself.

> Boasting is necessary, though it is not profitable; but I will go on to visions and revelations of the Lord. I know a man in Christ who fourteen years ago—whether in the body I do not know, or out of the body I do not know, God knows—such a man was caught up to the third heaven. And I know how such a man—whether in the body or apart from the body I do not know, God knows—was caught up into Paradise, and heard inexpressible words, which a man is not permitted to speak. On behalf of such a man will I boast; but on my own behalf I will not boast, except in regard to my weaknesses. For if I do wish to boast I shall not be foolish, for I shall be speaking the truth; but I refrain from this, so that no one may credit me with more than he sees in me or hears from me. And because of the surpassing greatness of the revelations, for this reason, to keep me from exalting myself, there was given me a thorn in the flesh, a messenger of Satan to buffet me—to keep me from exalting myself! [2 Corinthians 12:1-7]

Paul's prayers for healing were to no avail, so he finally rested in this wonderful thought:

And He said to me, "My grace is sufficient for you, for power is perfected in weakness." Most gladly, therefore, I will rather boast about my weaknesses, that the power of Christ may dwell in me. [2 Corinthians 12:9]

So it is today. Folks are often sick that God's strength may be manifested through their weakness. In that way God gets all of the glory.

CHASTENS THE SAINTS

First Corinthians is a letter of condemnation, not commendation. The church members had internal squabbles, condoned immorality, took one another to court, and misused their God-given gifts. But worst of all, they desecrated the Lord's Supper.

Therefore when you meet together, it is not to eat the Lord's Supper, for in your eating each one takes his own supper first; and one is hungry and another is drunk. What! Do you not have houses in which to eat and drink? Or do you despise the church of God, and shame those who have nothing? What shall I say to you? Shall I praise you? In this I will not praise you. [1 Corinthians 11:20-22]

Paul went on to explain to them that they were eating and drinking judgment to themselves.

For he who eats and drinks, eats and drinks judgment to himself, if he does not judge the body rightly. For this reason many among you are weak and sick, and a number sleep. [1 Corinthians 11:29-30]

God chastened the Corinthians because of that sin. The sudden death of Ananias and Sapphira (Acts 5:1-11) for lying to the Holy Spirit is another example. It is for illnesses from that cause that God provides the anointing service in James 5.

PROVIDES COMFORT

Have you ever noticed that people listen to your advice more carefully if you have already been through a particular circumstance yourself? That's just a part of our human nature. Jesus knows our circumstances, for even He was tested. "For we do not have a high priest who cannot sympathize with our weaknesses, but one who has been tempted in all things as we are, yet without sin" (Hebrews 4:15).

If you are now sick or suffering, it could be that God is actually preparing you to minister by being a vessel through whom He will comfort others. Your trial may later become the platform from which you minister.

Blessed be the God and Father of our Lord Jesus Christ, the Father of mercies and God of all comfort; who comforts us in all our affliction so that we may be able to comfort those who are in any affliction with the comfort with which we ourselves are comforted by God. [2 Corinthians 1:3-5]

ACCOMPLISHES GOD'S UNREVEALED PURPOSES

When all of our answers are exhausted and our curiosity is not satisfied, we can appeal to these special Scriptures.

It is the glory of God to conceal a matter, but the glory of kings is to search out a matter. [Proverbs 25:2]

The secret things belong to the Lord our God, but the things revealed belong to us and to our sons forever, that we may observe all the words of this law. [Deuteronomy 29:29]

To admit that God acts in ways that are beyond our reasoning and His written revelation does not beg the question. Frequently such Scriptures as those are our last court of appeal and should be just as satisfying as the more specific answers.

Several years ago I was in Chicago to attend a writing course. In the class was an evangelist named Ben. One morning between classes we were having coffee and discussing how Ben's life was different because he was blind. I do not remember all that was said but I did jot down one thought. Ben was asked how he became blind. He unhesitatingly replied, "I am blind by God's design."

It ultimately is "by God's design" that Ben or anyone else is sick or suffering. But God may choose not to show us why until we reach glory. What would God have us do while we suffer? The Scriptures give us a prescription.

A BIBLICAL PRESCRIPTION FOR THE PATIENT

When this material was first written I had never been seriously ill. I wrote from the platform of Scripture and common sense. Admittedly, I had never personally had the opportunity to test its usefulness.

Then I was leveled by hypoglycemia. There was terrible fear, a radical personality change, and at times uncontrollable crying —all for no apparent reason. For six agonizing months our family had no idea what caused those unexplainable phenomena. During that time I retreated over and over to the principles in this chapter.

Finally, after a five-hour glucose tolerance test, the doctor realized the source of my problem. Through exercise and a controlled diet the Lord has very graciously restored my full health. During those dark days, however, my only sustaining help came from applying the truths I now share. I trust they will be as helpful for you.

It would be ideal if we had one clear Scripture that said, "When you are sick, this is what you should do." Unfortunately there is none. So the following prescription is taken from various portions of God's Word.

First, acknowledge that God is sovereign and rest in that unshakable truth. God is in control of every moment whether in sickness or health. "See now that I, I am He, and there is no god besides Me; it is I who put to death and give life. I have wounded, and it is I who heal; and there is no one who can deliver from My hand" (Deuteronomy 32:39).

Second, remind yourself of the biblical reasons for sickness— those purposes God can accomplish through it.

Third, it is extremely important to determine if a sickness is because of continued sin in your life. Is God using your illness as chastisement? For most of us the answer will be no. But if your answer happens to be yes, confess your sin (1 John 1:9). It could be that the James 5 anointing service is for you. You may want to discuss it with your pastor.

Fourth, by faith commit the entire matter to the Lord. Pray for God's will to be done, seek His glory, and wait patiently for His response.

Fifth, seek professional medical attention. Never disregard or ignore God's normal means to restored health through medical experts. Do not presume upon God and wait too long or ignore your doctor altogether.

Sixth, recognize that it is not necessarily God's will for you to fully recover. Many of God's great servants were sick—Isaac, Jacob, Moses, Job, Daniel, Paul, Epaphroditus, and Timothy. They all eventually died.

Thank God for the circumstances in which He has placed you. "Always giving thanks for all things in the name of our Lord Jesus Christ to God, even the Father" (Ephesians 5:20). "In everything give thanks; for this is God's will for you in Christ Jesus" (1 Thessalonians 5:18).

You are not thanking God that you hurt, but rather that He is who He is and that He will work through your circumstances. In the end He will be glorified.

Next, as you pray, ask God for the faith and patience to endure and the wisdom to understand why (James 1:2-5). He promised that His Grace would be sufficient (2 Corinthians 12:9). Claim that reassuring scriptural promise for yourself and rest in it.

Finally, pray that your circumstances might be worked out for the glory of God. "Whether, then, you eat or drink or whatever you do, do all to the glory of God" (1 Corinthians 10:31). If that is not a continual part of your thinking, you will never have full victory in the midst of your circumstances.

So far we have not discussed prayer for healing. We can be assured that there is nothing wrong with asking. Paul asked three times to be healed (2 Corinthians 12:8). However, we need to be willing to prayerfully receive God's answer regardless of what it is.

The most appropriate word of wisdom I know of in that regard has been offered by Charles Wood. His wife fought several bouts with cancer. They had prayed often. He counsels, "In illness, I would pray for healing until God grants it or unless

124 / Divine Healing Today

or until He makes it plain that it is not His will and gives peace about it."[1] That is sound advice.

This prescription will not heal you. However, it will allow you to keep the right view of God and maintain a closer fellowship with Him. We can pray as did the Norwegian theologian Ole Hallesby:

> Lord, if it will be to Your glory, heal suddenly. If it will glorify You more, heal gradually; if it will glorify You even more, may your servant remain sick awhile; and if it will glorify Your name still more, take him to Yourself in heaven.

1. Charles R. Wood, "We Learned to Pray for Healing," *Moody Monthly*, November 1976, p. 157.

✦ 12 ✦

Monday Afternoon with
Joni Eareckson

Most people in America know the story of Joni Eareckson because of the vast amount of public exposure she has received, especially from her books, paintings, and public appearances. God is using her tremendously to minister to the disabled.

But the public doesn't see the "day by day" Joni. Most people do not understand her struggle to do the ordinary things of life, such as bathing or eating. They only see her as a "superstar."

I visited Joni at her modest Woodland Hills home overlooking the San Fernando Valley in Southern California. Joni was in bed because of pressure sores, but she very graciously spent an afternoon with me.

DICK: Do you believe the faith-healing movement and its message are misleading?

JONI: I recently flew to a speaking engagement in St. Louis, and during the flight I got involved in a conversation with a young stewardess who just had the love of Jesus written all over her face. She was one of the most bubbly, effervescent persons I've ever met. She was obviously a new Christian in love with the Lord. She told me, "Joni, I just could not serve a God who did not want everybody healed—a God whose will it was not to heal everybody."

My comment to her was, "Well, obviously, just from a casual observation of our world, we can see that it is not God's will that everyone be healed, because everyone is not healed. Man cannot resist God's will, and if it was God's purpose and design and will that all men be healed, nothing could stop that. We would see evidences of it in the world around us, but we don't. So it's obviously not God's will that everybody be healed."

Her next comment to me was something to the effect of, "Well, doesn't our faith have anything to do with it?" I guess that's one thing that would be good for us to discuss, because people, aside from having an incorrect view of God's kingdom and an incorrect hermeneutic, will tend to pull out certain portions of Scripture, little verses here and there that speak of faith, and base a whole theology around that faith.

I see faith as merely a vehicle through which God's grace works. Others, of the persuasion of that stewardess, perhaps see faith as the club that we hold over God's head, or the string we have to pull for God to work. In my view, that does not seem to be faith; it seems to be presumption. It almost makes God a puppet.

DICK: Have you ever gone to a faith-healing service?

JONI: Frankly, I went to a couple of Kathryn Kuhlman's meetings. I think the idea is wrong in a very subtle way in that it fosters the mentality that the stewardess had—that God's purpose in redeeming mankind is primarily to make us happy, healthy, and our lives free from trouble. Pursuing those kinds of avenues of grasping at straws and pulling levers to manipulate God or twisting His arm or trimming Him down to our size—those are very desperate attempts to get our wants met and our prayers answered the way we think we ought to have them answered. His purpose in redeeming us is to conform us to Christ's image, and we often forget that.

DICK: When you went, did you get in the healing line?

JONI: Yes. As I recall, it was at the Hilton in Washington. It was so packed and so crowded and I was way in the back. There were chairs all around and none of us could move. I mean we were all wedged up one against another.

There were people with chairs, people with walkers, people with crutches, just like myself. You must understand, Dick, I got to the point where I was inventing sins to confess. I wanted to make sure that everything was so up front with God. Way down deep I felt a little foolish being there, but I felt it was necessary for me to be foolish in front of God, in front of all those people.

It was necessary for me to prostrate myself and make myself totally and openly vulnerable, not only before Him but before those people. And I had others praying for me as I went to that meeting.

I'd been anointed with oil already. I had had countless numbers of people lay hands on me. I thought, "That's really good because that means all the proper stuff is being done." All that stuff you think is supposed to happen — pastors laying hands on you, oil, prayers, and sins that I confessed. I did everything. And I went there believing that God had been paving the way and preparing the scene and that I was just going to be able to wheel right onto the platform and that would truly be it!

But nothing happened. I could not understand for the longest time why my hands and my legs were not getting the message my mind was telling them. I remember looking at my appendages as though they were something separate from who I was and what I thought. My heart and my mind said, *You're healed, body!* I wanted to make sure that I believed with a capital *B*.

DICK: Had you been programmed by reading some of the faith-healing literature?

JONI: Yes. It was a matter of *my* faith—working that faith, getting it nice and exercised and in tip-top condition. I really believed! And yet, my hands and feet did not respond to what I knew was true. Then I began to see that either God was playing some kind of monstrous, cruel joke on me, that I was the brunt of some divine comedy, or my view of Scripture was wrong.

I could not believe that God was playing a joke on me. I'd seen God work in other ways in my life and believed the Scriptures. I just knew that was not part of His nature and character. He is not the God of confusion or cruel tricks. So I resolved that the problem must be with me, but I knew it wasn't my faith. I believed so much. I had called people and told them, "Watch for me on your doorstep tomorrow. I'm going to be bounding up your sidewalk, running." I really left myself open. I believed, so I knew that the fault could not lie with my faith.

It had to lie with my wrong view of Scripture. That's when I began to look all the way back to the Garden of Eden, at the very root of suffering, disease, illness, injury, and death. I saw that sickness began with sin and, as I recounted in *A Step Further*, I very slowly and meticulously began to piece together God's redemptive flow of history throughout the Bible until I began to see it all fit together. When I got to the New Testament, I suddenly began to understand the miracles, the healing, and all the excitement when Jesus was down here on earth.

It made great sense that suffering was supposed to be part of the fabric and the fiber of God's redeeming mankind. And even after salvation, suffering was supposed to fit into the fabric and the fiber of the redemptive story. When Jesus came to deal with sin and sin's results, He put the process into motion and began to reverse the effects of sin and all of its results. But in doing so He was only laying the foundation. However, the world is still fallen; it still has people dying; it still has natural catastrophes and people getting sick, and will until He comes back.

It helped me so to read through the Old Testament. As I read through all of those promises under the Old Covenant—how the eyes of the blind were opened, the ears of the deaf were unstopped, and the anointed of the Lord obtained joy and gladness, I slowly began to see that when Jesus came, that was just the beginning. It really wasn't the entire picture. As we know, He's coming back, not as a humble servant but as reigning King. He will complete the kingdom and usher in all those glorious promises.

I guess that is why I don't mind being in a wheelchair and putting up with suffering. If it means more people being granted entrance to the kingdom of God, more folks being a part of His family, it all has meaning. To suffer without a reason is to suffer for nothing. That would be painful.

DICK: Let's come back to the stewardess. How did your conversation with her turn out?

JONI: The conversation that I had with that stewardess was disturbing because it was truly, in capsule form, what is occurring in churches all over the country. When I got off the plane at the airport, I was greeted by my sponsors. They had brought with them a young woman who had broken her neck in an automobile accident a year before. She was a quadriplegic much like myself. She had come to the point where she could trust God with it and accept it.

But someone had told her that it was God's will for her to be healed. Well, she had believed and believed and worked hard and followed all those scriptural injunctions and had done everything that she thought was necessary—and yet she was not healed. That just catapulted her into depression; it was hurting her view of God.

In her thinking He was becoming an ogre up there who was playing monstrous jokes on people down here. And then she was told, "Now wait a minute; your depression isn't showing a life of faith. And in fact, young woman, your depression is nothing more than sheer sin." Oh, it was cruel, awfully cruel!

Her comment to that person was, "Well, look at Joni. She loves the Lord and has a close walk with Christ, yet the Lord has not chosen to heal her."

She was told, "Well, Joni has resigned herself never to be healed. That's why Joni's not healed."

She was just so anxious to hear it from the horse's mouth. Did I ever get depressed? Did I believe it was God's will? Have I resigned myself to never being on my feet?

Fresh from that other conversation with the stewardess, my first statement to her was, "No, I have not resigned myself never to be healed." Some people on one end of the spectrum say that God never miraculously heals. They almost put God's actions in a box. And on the other end of the spectrum certain people say that God wants everybody healed. They, too, try to put God in a box. So I told her, "No, I have never resigned myself to never be healed. I've opened all those doors. I've left them open. But it's God's responsibility; it's no longer mine. If I have a proper view of Scripture and a high view of God, then it's at His discretion."

But I do believe, as I told her, that healing is the exception to the rule; the rule being that God will not always miraculously heal in this day and age any more than He will miraculously raise people from the dead or walk on water. Those things just aren't occurring.

I told her that I often do get depressed. For instance, I'm in bed right now with a couple of stubborn little pressure sores. I've been down in bed for a number of months. It's been very discouraging and at times depressing. I've had people say that they're praying for my healing.

The young woman asked me with a curious look on her face. "Well, don't you think that's sin?"

I said, "If I allowed these emotions to alter my view of God, that would be sin. But it is not sin in that my view of God has not changed."

However, I am human. He knows my frame and remembers that I am but dust. He's made me a being with real tears. Emotionally, I'm not going to be real happy about lying in bed for three months, but that has not altered my view of God. The depression that I am experiencing is simply indigenous to what it means to be human. Some depression is just a part of what it means to face the everyday bumps and bruises of being human, whether you are a believer or an unbeliever. However, despair for the Christian is not necessary because we have hope—the hope of Christ setting up a new order of things.

DICK: That's a good distinction between the word *depression,* a part of our humanness, and *despair,* which should never be a part of our redemptive relationship with Christ.

JONI: It's so wonderful. I did despair when I was first injured—I just didn't know how to fit it all together. I had no idea that God was there; that He cared; that He was in control and that I didn't have to worry; that it was not an accident; that He had a planned purpose and had resurrection power to give me. I just didn't know all that. So in the early months of my disability, yes, I did despair. I thought there was no hope. But Christians should never have to despair, although they might get depressed.

DICK: Have you ever analyzed the stages of your thinking from the time you were a teen and first crippled to the point where you are now? Have you noticed any marked stages that you've gone through?

JONI: Well, I think I followed the classic example of anybody who comes to the point of finally accepting their disabilities. There are five steps: the classic stages of shock, denial, anger, bargaining, and acceptance.

At first, yes—I was shocked and totally disbelieving. It's curious, Dick. I saw my body paralyzed, but it never clicked that this is the way it would always be. It wasn't that I refused to think about it; something was not connecting. It never clicked because it was all a shock. And then came anger. "God, how could You allow something like this to happen to me?"

Again, that's another thing that's always been curious to me—why we lay the blame on God. What is it about Him? It must be inherent in our rebellious natures that we should lay the blame on Him. We never really put the blame on man's initial rebellion; we throw the responsibility on God, not Satan. True to our human nature, such is the nature of the beast. It seems as if we can't accept responsibility for anything.

Then I went through denial. "This is not the way it should be. God, I just know that you're going to get me up on my feet." After I went through the bargaining routine I finally came to the point where I accepted it. But not acceptance in the sense of hopeless resignation—"I guess this is the best that can be done with it, so I'll just accept it and go on"—a sense of self-pitying martyrdom. I'm talking about acceptance where you embrace what God has given you and take it with thanksgiving. I think that's genuine acceptance and that only a Christian can do that.

I think many unbelievers accept their situation with a kind of a martyr complex or stoic resignation. But only Christians can embrace it with thanksgiving, knowing that they are receiving from the hand of God something that is not only for His glory but for their own good.

Back to the story with the young quadriplegic. We talked and chatted a bit about the kingdom of God. Whenever someone asks me about healing today, I'll first start talking about the kingdom and why Christ came and what those miracles were all about. I don't think you can give the answers to the questions until you give them the framework, the structure in which you can couch your answers. We talked about depression a bit more before I went to my hotel room.

The next morning I got up to speak at a ladies' luncheon— there were 1,000 women there—and I talked about the nature and character of God and our view of Him in the middle of our pain and problems. I prefaced my talk with the fact that I was depressed. And I was. It was about a week and a half ago and, as I told you, I was really struggling with being in bed and feeling ugly and adding a few pounds, because when I get down, I eat.

But anyway, I was describing that to them because I wanted those people to understand that this is not some carefully constructed view of Scripture that I pieced together years ago.

Well, after I spoke I went back to the hotel room to lie down, because I had to get off my bed sore. Then the phone rang. It was a woman who wanted to talk with me. I put the phone to my ear and she began by saying, "Joni, I have a word of knowledge for you from the Lord." She went on as people will often do when they say words of knowledge, "My daughter. . . ."—as if God were actually speaking. She wanted to say, "My daughter, [and something to do with the effect that] your sin is keeping you from Me and healing. This depression that you have is blocking My fellowship with you."

I really had to bite my tongue at the end of her "word of knowledge." I said, "Thank you for calling and sharing your opinion." I just thought about how cruel and unfair that lady was! She used a convenient spiritual loophole to express her opinion. If you want to give me your opinion, call it your opinion. I didn't say that to her, but I was really boiling. Again, it goes right back to the stewardess and the girl in the wheelchair. When we trim God down to our size, somewhere along the line we've lost the high view of God that the men and women of the Bible had. We fit Him into our convenient box.

DICK: Oftentimes people look at you and imagine that you live a happy-go-lucky, normal life at home. How do you handle daily problems?

JONI: I suppose the problem that I can best talk about right now is this problem of having to be in bed with this bedsore, feeling that my world doesn't go beyond that back fence, sensing that my prayers don't go past the ceiling, or looking into a mirror—dirty hair and no make-up and sheets that smell of alcohol and antiseptic. To me it's a lesson in learning to effectively appropriate God's Word all over again.

I learned long ago that the key to going forward in my Christian walk is to systematically and intelligently approach God's Word, break it down into some understandable portions speaking, let's say, of depression or trials or grace, and memorize them.

That still holds true today. I have to sidestep the feelings of my limitations, the sensations of my prayers bouncing off the ceiling, the impulses, the emotions, and the vacillation. I purpose in my mind, which I suppose is an act of faith, not to listen to my feelings, but instead to listen to the Word of God. So it's actually a volitional act; it's an intention of the will that I'm not going to let those feelings and emotions rip my faith apart and alter my view of God.

I'm going to accept them for what they are—emotions and feelings—and then continue on the straight line of listening to the Word of God. The Word of God tells me that all things fit together in a pattern for good. It doesn't say all things are good, but it says all things fit together for good. I'm going to listen to the Word of God when it says to welcome trials as friends and in everything give thanks. I think it's a systematic approach to His Word that makes the difference.

DICK: Don't those people who are sick often ask and need to know why they are sick and what God's reasons are for their sickness?

JONI: Yes, or they ask, Why am I not healed? It's important to answer that if we, the church, are going to minister to people with severe disabilities or spend time with them, discipling or whatever.

Sometimes people will pray for healing for an aunt who is terminally ill or a husband who is dying of cancer. They just know God is going to raise that individual up. Then when that person dies, they rejoice because he's experienced what they call the epitome of real healing. That's clearly a loophole—a spiritual loophole—a very convenient out.

DICK: But there's an element of truth to it. That is what is so deceiving, isn't it?

JONI: Yes, because that is not what those people mean. They are praying that this or that person be healed. In fact, they would not even want to think, for fear of showing lack of faith, that there might be a possibility that real healing means death.

DICK: In light of your experience and all the people you correspond with, what are the most important questions that really need to be answered for people who find themselves sick or suffering, or in circumstances that they will never be able to change?

JONI: I think the one that's hounding most people is, What responsibility does God have? How could God, a good God, allow suffering and evil in this world? And second, How much of my potential healing is up to me? Where does my faith fit into it? What is God's involvement?

We sort of covered the first. Maybe we can talk a little bit more about the second. People have a tough time being convinced that when Jesus said, "Your faith has made you well," He was really talking about salvation in those particular portions of Scripture. I believe that He was; the healing was merely an evidence of being made well spiritually.

But people still believe that it's a matter of exercising their faith. They still believe that those portions of Scripture, for instance, where Jesus says, "If you have faith the size of a grain of mustard seed, you say to this mountain, be moved, and it will move," place all the responsibility on them.

Sometimes I think that God would read their heart intent; but then perhaps it is in the providence of God that they should be sorely mistaken so that they might be moved to take a closer look at Scripture.

Take, for example, that young stewardess. What will that dear girl do when her husband gets deathly ill? What will she do? My heart goes out to her in one sense. But yet, in another sense, I can see that God would want her to be sadly, sadly disappointed, so that as with me it would press her to go back to Scripture for a second, harder look. I feel for those folks. I can see myself, as I once was, in that position. I guess that makes it all the more imperative that people, like you and others who are in a position of sharing God's truth should be accurate. It puts a great challenge before you.

Joni's personal insights into sickness and suffering have been gleaned since her teen years as she has depended on God to sustain her through the trials of being a quadriplegic. I hope she has ministered to you through her special life and spiritual insights on suffering and sickness.[1]

1. To learn more of Joni and her struggles to be victorious, read her two books, *Joni* and *A Step Further* (Zondervan).

♦ 13 ♦

The Terminal Disease

Can you imagine visiting your doctor for a minor problem and having him diagnose your ailment as a potentially terminal disease? But far better it is to discover it while you can still receive treatment.

In the early thirties my grandfather complained of a skin irritation on his left ear. At the insistence of my grandmother, he scheduled an appointment with his doctor.

Much to my grandfather's shock, his physician discovered the inflammation to be cancerous. Surgery was scheduled for the following day, and although his ear was amputated, the operation prevented the cancer from spreading to his brain. The good news overshadowed the bad.

Two thousand years ago a certain man found himself in a similar situation. He suffered from obvious paralysis, but Jesus announced that he was afflicted with a more serious problem—a potentially terminal disease.

And when He had come back to Capernaum several days afterward, it was heard that He was at home. And many were gathered together, so that there was no longer room, even near the door; and He was speaking the word to them. And they came, bringing to Him a paralytic, carried by four men. And being unable to get to Him because of the crowd, they removed the roof above Him; and when they had dug an opening, they let down the pallet on which the paralytic was lying. And Jesus seeing their faith said to the paralytic, "My son, your sins are forgiven." But there were some of the scribes sitting there and reasoning in their hearts, "Why does this man speak that way? He is blaspheming; who can forgive sins but God alone?" And immediately Jesus, aware in His spirit that they were reasoning that way within themselves, said to them, "Why are you reasoning about these things in your hearts? Which is easier, to say to the paralytic, 'Your sins are forgiven'; or to say, 'Arise, and take up your pallet and walk'? But in order that you may know that the Son of Man has authority on earth to forgive sins"—He said to the paralytic—"I say to you, rise, take up your pallet and go home." And he rose and immediately took up the pallet and went out in the sight of all; so that they were all amazed and were glorifying God, saying "We have never seen anything like this." [Mark 2:1-12]

That paralytic was blessed with four friends who had heard about Christ's healing ministry. When He returned to Capernaum they brought the paralytic to be healed. I'm sure they thought they could do nothing more wonderful than bring their friend to be healed. Then he would be well and work alongside of them.

As usual the crowd was enormous, and it was impossible to reach Jesus. So intense was their desire to see their friend healed that they dug through the earthen roof of the house and lowered the paralytic directly in front of Jesus (Luke 5:19).

Jesus was well known for the unexpected, and this occasion would be no exception. Instead of saying, "Arise and walk!" the Savior announced, "Your sins are forgiven."

The man thought that his most serious defect was paralysis, but Jesus diagnosed his deepest problem as sin. What a shock! Paralysis is temporal—it ceases at death; but sin is eternal—it results in separation from God forever. That is why Jesus dealt with sin first.

Jesus' clinical technique was ahead of its time. The *holistic* approach to medicine has only recently come into vogue. Holistic medicine assumes that most illnesses are, at least in part, the product of psychological or even spiritual disharmony.[1] The Great Physician knew that and truly ministered to the whole man.

It was not until the Pharisees challenged Christ's authority to forgive sin (Mark 2:6-8) that Jesus actually healed the paralytic. And then it was so they might know that the Son of Man had authority on earth to forgive sins. But note this carefully: although the man eventually lost his newfound health through death, he is this very day experiencing eternal life because his sins were forgiven.

It could be that we, as the paralytic and his faithful friends, have been focusing *only* on the physical. Christ reminds us that God's concern is primarily for the spiritual. Our greatest problem is sin, not sickness.

Romans 3:9-18 pictures sin as an ugly cancer that spreads throughout the body. It affects our mind (v. 11), mouth (v. 14), throat (v. 13), feet (v. 15), tongue (v. 13), eyes (v. 18), and lips (v. 13).

Unfortunately, no one is immune. We are all afflicted. "There is none righteous, not even one; there is none who understands, there is none who seeks for God" (Romans 3:10-11). "For all have sinned and fall short of the glory of God" (v. 23).

Sin affects our soul as cancer affects our body. Dr. Paul Brand and Philip Yancey picture cancer in the physical world in this way:

Like many Indian beggars, the woman was emaciated, with sunken cheeks and eyes and bony limbs. But, paradoxically, a huge mass of plump skin, round and sleek like a sausage, was growing from her side. It lay beside her like a formless baby, connected to her by a broad bridge of skin. The woman had exposed her flank with its grotesque deformity to give her an advantage in the rivalry for pity. Though I saw her only briefly, I felt sure that the growth was a lipoma, a tumor of fat cells. It was a part of her and yet not, as if some surgeon had carved a hunk of fat out of a three hundred pound person, wrapped it in live skin, and deftly sewed it on this woman. She was starving; she feebly

1. Tim Hackler, "Holistic Medicine," *Mainliner,* February 1981, pp. 92-96.

held up a spidery hand for alms. But her tumor was thriving, nearly equaling the weight of the rest of her body. It gleamed in the sun, exuding health, sucking life from her.[2]

Like the tumor that sucked life from the Indian beggarwoman, sin snatches life from the spiritually impoverished. Jesus Christ is the only cure.

Jesus said to him, "I am the way, and the truth, and the life; no one comes to the Father, but through Me." [John 14:6]

And there is salvation in no one else; for there is no other name under heaven that has been given among men, by which we must be saved. [Acts 4:12]

Perhaps you are one who fully understands that sin is your greatest problem but don't know what to do about it. Listen to Paul's words.

If you confess with your mouth Jesus as Lord, and believe in your heart that God raised Him from the dead, you shall be saved; for with the heart man believes, resulting in righteousness, and with the mouth he confesses, resulting in salvation. For the Scripture says, "Whoever believes in Him will not be disappointed." For there is no distinction between Jew and Greek; for the same Lord is Lord of all, abounding in riches for all who call upon Him; for "whoever will call upon the name of the Lord will be saved." [Romans 10:9-13]

For by grace you have been saved though faith; and that not of yourselves, it is the gift of God; not as a result of works, that no one should boast. For we are His workmanship, created in Christ Jesus for good works, which God prepared beforehand, that we should walk in them. [Ephesians 2:8-10]

In Matthew 11:28-30 Jesus gives this invitation:

Come to Me, all who are weary and heavy-laden, and I will give you rest. Take My yoke upon you, and learn from Me, for I am gentle and

2. Paul Brand and Philip Yancey, *Fearfully and Wonderfully Made* (Grand Rapids: Zondervan, 1980), pp. 57-58.

humble in heart; and you shall find rest for your souls. For my yoke is easy, and My load is light.

Salvation is extended to you as you read this. If you are weary and heavy-laden with sin, Christ is offering you eternal rest. But you must turn from your sin and come to Christ as your Savior (11:28). Submit yourself to His lordship by entering the yoke with Him (v. 29). He will carry your burden of sin, and eternal life will be yours.

If that is your present need, bow your head right where you are and invite Jesus Christ to be your Savior and Lord. Pray in your own words—He will understand.

If you receive Christ, the promise of John 5:24 will be yours to claim: "Truly, truly, I say to you, he who hears My Word, and believes Him who sent Me, has eternal life, and does not come into judgment, but has passed out of death into life."

Contact a Bible-teaching church in your area. God will use that church to feed you from His Word and build you up in the faith.

I would pray for you as Paul prayed for the Ephesian believers:

I bow my knees before the Father from whom every family in heaven and on earth derives its name, that He would grant you, according to the riches of His glory, to be strengthened with power through His spirit in the inner man; so that Christ may dwell in your hearts through faith; and that you, being rooted and grounded in love, may be able to comprehend with all the saints what is the breadth and length and height and depth, and to know the love of Christ which surpasses knowledge, that you may be filled up to all the fulness of God. [Ephesians 3:14-19]

Appendix 1

The Old Testament Healing Record

The Old Testament bridges the time from creation to B.C. 400. It is naive to assume that every instance of illness or healing was recorded. However, it does seem reasonable that the majority of special cases are included in the divine record. The central statement on divine healing was written by Moses in Deuteronomy 32:39:

> See now that I, I am He,
> And there is no god besides Me;
> It is I who put to death and give life.
> I have wounded, and it is I who heal;
> And there is no one who can deliver from My hand.

The testimony is clear: *God is ultimately responsible for life or death and health or sickness.*

The following material characterizes the ministry of divine healing in the Old Testament.

141

GOD AFFLICTED

God physically afflicted as well as He physically healed. For example:

Genesis 32:22-32—Jacob
Exodus 4:6-7—Moses
Exodus 12:29-30—Firstborn of Egypt
Leviticus 10:1-2—Abihu and Nadab
Numbers 12:1-15—Miriam
2 Samuel 12:1-23—Infant son of David
2 Kings 5:20-27—Gehazi
2 Kings 19:35—Sennacherib's army
2 Chronicles 21:16-20—Jehoram
2 Chronicles 26:16-21—Uzziah
Ezekiel 24:16—Ezekiel's wife
Daniel 4:28-37—Nebuchadnezzar

HEALING METHODS VARIED

God honored, and at times personally used, various techniques to physically heal.

1. **Prayer**
   Genesis 20:1-18—Abraham
   Numbers 12:1-15—Moses
   1 Samuel 1:19-20—Hannah
   1 Kings 17:17-24—Elijah
2. **Hand into his bosom**
   Exodus 4:6-7—Moses
3. **According to God's predetermined time limit**
   Daniel 4:28-37—Seven years
4. **Dipping seven times in the Jordan River**
   2 Kings 5:1-14—Naaman
5. **Unexplained actions**
   1 Kings 17:17-24—Elijah
   2 Kings 4:18-37—Elisha
6. **Without anything**
   Genesis 21:1-2—Sarah
   Genesis 29:31 —Leah
   Genesis 30:22—Rachel

7. **Combination of events**
   1 Kings 17:17-24—Prayer and unexplained actions
   2 Kings 4:18-37—Prayer and unexplained actions
   2 Kings 20:1-11—Prayer and medicine
8. **Looking at an elevated serpent**
   Numbers 21:4-9—Israel
9. **Plague checked, but no physical healing**
   Numbers 16:1-50—Incense offered
   Numbers 25:1-9—Two people killed
   1 Samuel 5:6, 9, 12—Obedience
   2 Samuel 24:1-17—Predetermined time limit

SIN-RELATED SICKNESS

Some physical affliction was directly given because of personal sin, although the person physically afflicted was not always the sinner.

1. **The sinner went unpunished**
   Exodus 32:22-32—Aaron
   Numbers 12:1-15—Aaron
2. **The sinner was punished**
   Leviticus 10:1-2—Nadab and Abihu
   Numbers 12:1-15—Miriam
   Numbers 16:1-50—Korah
   Daniel 4:28-37—Nebuchadnezzar
3. **Someone other than the sinner was punished**
   Genesis 12:17—Household of Pharaoh
   Genesis 20:1-18—Household of Abimelech
   2 Samuel 12:1-23—Child of David and Bathsheba
   2 Samuel 24:1-17—House of Israel

UNEXPLAINABLE SICKNESS

Genesis 21:1-2—Sarah
Genesis 27:1—Isaac
Genesis 32:22-32—Jacob
1 Samuel 1:19-20—Hannah
2 Samuel 4:4—Mephibosheth
1 Kings 17:17-24—Widow's son
2 Kings 4:18-37—Shunammite's son

GOD HEALED UNBELIEVERS

Genesis 12:10-20—Pharaoh's household
Genesis 20:1-18—Abimelech
2 Kings 5:1-14—Naaman
Daniel 4:28-37—Nebuchadnezzar

GOD RESTORED LIFE

In the Old Testament, only three people were resuscitated.

1 Kings 17:17-24—Son of the widow of Zarephath
2 Kings 4:18-37—Son of the Shunammite woman
2 Kings 13:21—Unnamed man whose body touched the bones of Elisha

SATAN CAUSED SICKNESS

God mentioned Satan as an agent for sickness *only once.* Job 1-2

SAINTS WERE SICK

Some of the greatest Old Testament saints were ill, but not directly because of personal sin.

Genesis 27:1—Isaac (uncured)
Genesis 32:25—Jacob (uncured)
Genesis 48:1—Jacob (uncured)
Exodus 4:6-7—Moses (cured)
1 Kings 14:4—Ahijah (uncured)
2 Kings 13:14—Elisha (uncured)
Job 1-2; 42:10—Job (cured)
Daniel 8:27—Daniel (cured)

Appendix 2

The Gospel Healing Record

Never in human history were so many people healed from such a multitude of diseases in so short a time as during Christ's public ministry. It has not been repeated. Christ's healing ministry was truly unique and remains unequaled.

PURPOSES FOR HEALING

There were various purposes for Christ's healing ministry and all of them primarily contributed to authenticate the person of Jesus as the true Messiah. The healing miracles were never performed *merely* for their physical benefit.

Matthew 8:17—To fulfill the messianic prophecy in Isaiah 53:4

Matthew 9:6 (also Mark 2:10; Luke 5:24)—That people would know that Christ had the authority to forgive sins

Matthew 11:2-19 (also Luke 7:18-23)—To authenticate the messianic ministry for the imprisoned John

Matthew 12:15-21—To fulfill the messianic prophecy in Isaiah 42:1-4

John 9:3—That the works of God might be displayed in Christ

John 11:4—For the glory of God through Christ

John 20:30-31—That men might believe that Jesus is Christ

Acts 2:22—To serve as God's authentication of Christ

HEALING HAD PURPOSE

Although Jesus' miracles were abundant, He did not perform them indiscriminately or always heal everyone who needed healing (see John 5:3-5); nor did He perform signs upon request (see Matthew 12:38-40) or use His powers to avoid the cross (see Matthew 26:52-53). Miracles were always directed toward the purposes documented above.

Matthew 4:3-4	Matthew 27:40
Matthew 12:38-40	Mark 6:5
Matthew 16:1-4	Luke 11:16
Matthew 26:52-53	John 5:3-5

HEALING WAS IMMEDIATE

With three exceptions, all of Jesus' healings were instantaneous. Absolutely no recuperative period was needed, for the afflicted were immediately returned to complete health. There were no relapses or misunderstandings about being healed.

Matthew 8:3	Matthew 9:29-30	Mark 3:1-6
Matthew 8:13	Matthew 15:28	Mark 7:33-35
Matthew 8:15	Matthew 15:30-31	Luke 13:13
Matthew 9:6-7	Matthew 17:18	John 4:53
Matthew 9:22	Matthew 20:34	John 5:8-9

CERTAIN HEALINGS WERE TIME-DELAYED

The three delays in total healing involved *minutes* only. The men involved were totally healed.

Mark 8:22-26	Luke 17:11-19	John 9:1-7

HEALINGS WERE ABUNDANT

Jesus' miracles were abundant and unlimited in number and scope.

Matthew 4:23-25	Mark 1:32-34	John 6:2
Matthew 8:16	Mark 3:7-11	John 7:31
Matthew 9:35	Luke 6:17-19	John 12:37
Matthew 12:15	Luke 7:21	John 20:30
Matthew 14:35-36	Luke 9:11	John 21:25
Matthew 15:30-31		

HEALING IN ABSENTIA

Jesus' physical presence was unnecessary for healing to occur.

Matthew 8:5-13	Luke 7:1-10
Matthew 15:21-28	John 4:46-54

HEALING METHODS VARIED

As with Old Testament healings, Jesus used a variety of methods to heal. Remember, it was the power of God that healed—there was nothing magical or cure-producing in the method itself.

1. **Christ touched**
   Matthew 8:15   Matthew 20:34   Luke 13:13
2. **Christ spoke**
   Matthew 9:6-7   Mark 10:52   John 5:8-9
3. **The afflicted touched Christ's cloak**
   Matthew 9:20-22   Matthew 14:36   Luke 8:44
4. **Christ used spittle**
   Mark 8:22-26
5. **Christ plugged a man's ears with His fingers and placed spittle on his tongue**
   Mark 7:33-35
6. **Christ anointed with clay**
   John 9:6

CHRIST APPROVED DOCTORS

Jesus recognized the normal means of physical healing—a doctor and medicine.

> Matthew 9:12—"It is not those who are healthy who need a physician, but those who are sick."
> Luke 10:25-37—The Samaritan used oil, wine, and bandages to help the abandoned Jew.

HEALING FOR GOD'S GLORY

Although sickness can result directly from personal sin, as evidenced in the Old Testament, nowhere in the gospel accounts is sickness attributed directly to personal sin. However, it is stated twice that sickness occurred that God could be glorified.

> John 9:1-41—Man with congenital blindness
> John 11:1-53—Lazarus

CHRIST'S HEALING MINISTRY WAS UNIQUE

It is stated emphatically that in history there was never a healing ministry like Christ's ministry.

Matthew 9:32-33	Luke 10:24
Mark 2:12	John 9:32

CHRIST SHUNNED ACCLAIM

Jesus went out of His way to avoid public approval or reward for His healing miracles. In Luke 10:20 the disciples were told explicitly not to rejoice in the power they had been given, but to rejoice over the fact that their names were recorded in heaven.

Matthew 8:4	Mark 1:44	Mark 8:26
Matthew 9:30	Mark 5:43	Luke 5:14
Matthew 12:16	Mark 7:36	Luke 8:56

HEALINGS WERE UNDENIABLE

The spectator reaction to Christ's healings was phenomenal. Everyone, including His enemies, was amazed, astounded, and unable to deny or discredit the miracles.

Matthew 9:1-8	Mark 3:6	Luke 11:14-15
Matthew 9:33-34	Mark 3:10	Luke 18:43
Matthew 12:23-24	Mark 5:20	John 9:1-41
Matthew 15:31	Mark 7:37	John 11:47-48
Mark 2:12		

REACTIONS WERE NATIONAL

The reaction was nationwide. Mark 1:45 describes the fact that the news of Christ's healing ministry spread to such an extent that He could no longer enter a city. Even though He remained in unpopulated areas, people came to Him from *everywhere.*

Matthew 4:23-25	Matthew 9:35	Matthew 19:2
Matthew 9:26	Matthew 14:35	Mark 1:45
Matthew 9:31	Matthew 15:30	Mark 6:2

HEALING DID NOT SAVE

Christ's miracles were undeniable but did not necessarily lead to faith.

1. **They were undeniable**
   John 3:2   John 7:34-46   John 11:47-48
2. **They did not lead to faith**
   Matthew 11:21-23   John 6:26-30
   Matthew 12:38-45   John 12:37-43
   Luke 10:12-15

CHRIST HEALED UNBELIEVERS

Wherever He healed the multitudes it can be assumed that most, if not all, were unbelievers.

Matthew 8:1-4—A leper
Luke 17:11-19—Ten lepers
John 5:1-9—A lame man by the pool

FAITH NOT NECESSARY

A personal faith was *not* a necessary requirement to receive healing. In addition to the following, it is obvious that Lazarus, Jairus's daughter, and the widow's son were incapable of displaying faith. Yet, they were raised from the dead.

Matthew 8:14	Matthew 20:30	Luke 17:14
Matthew 9:32	Mark 7:35	Luke 22:51
Matthew 12:13	Mark 8:22	John 5:8
Matthew 12:22	Luke 14:4	John 9:1

ANOTHER'S FAITH HONORED

At times, Christ healed when faith was displayed by someone other than the one afflicted. Note especially Matthew 17:19-20. The disciples had been unable to cast out a demon and came to Jesus privately for further instruction. He informed them that they were unsuccessful because of their lack of faith. The parallel passage in Mark 9 adds that prayer would have been successful (see 9:29). Those who claim that a person is not healed because of his own lack of faith need to be alerted.

Matthew 8:10-11	Mark 2:1-5	John 4:50
Matthew 9:2	Mark 9:23-24	
Matthew 15:28	Luke 8:50	

FAITH OF THE AFFLICTED HONORED

Occasionally the faith of the afflicted one is commended.

Matthew 9:22	Matthew 9:29	Mark 10:52

HEALINGS WERE NOT PREARRANGED

1. **He healed from the beginning of His ministry (Matthew 4:23-25) to the end (John 11:1-44).**
2. **Often Jesus approached the person.**
   Luke 13:10-17   John 5:1-9

3. **Jesus always healed during the normal course of His ministry.**

Matthew 9:27-31   Luke 13:10-17
Matthew 12:10-14   John 5:1-9

SATAN CAUSED SICKNESS

Not all sickness is directly caused by Satan or demons, but those who are possessed by demons are liable to have physical infirmities. Luke 13:10-17 is the classic example—a lady bound by Satan (possibly through a demon) was doubled over for eighteen years.

Matthew 4:24   Matthew 17:14-18
Matthew 8:16-17   Mark 1:32-34
Matthew 9:32-33   Mark 9:25
Matthew 12:22   Luke 8:2
Matthew 15:21-28   Luke 13:10-17

HEAVENLY HEALING POWER

Because Christ had voluntarily abandoned the *independent* exercise of His divine attributes, His healing power came from God the Father.

Matthew 12:28—He cast out demons by the Spirit of God.
Luke 5:17—"And the power of the Lord was present for Him to perform healing."
Luke 11:20—He cast out demons by the finger of God.
John 5:19—"The Son can do nothing of Himself."
Acts 2:22—"Signs which God performed through Him."
Acts 10:38—Christ healed because God was with Him.

HEALING BY DISCIPLES

People other than Christ healed in the gospel accounts.

Matthew 10:1-15—Going only to the lost sheep of the house of Israel (see 10:6), all the disciples' needs were to be met supernaturally by God. They were to take nothing on their preaching and healing excursions.
Luke 10:1-16—The seventy others were commissioned similarly to the twelve.

Appendix 3

The Acts Healing Record

HEALING TECHNIQUES VARIED

The healing techniques varied in Acts as they did in the Old Testament and the gospels.

1. **By command**
   Acts 3:6   Acts 14:8-10
2. **By being in the healer's shadow**
   Acts 5:15
3. **By touching a cloth from the healer's body**
   Acts 19:11-12
4. **By prayer and laying on of hands**
   Acts 28:8-9

HEALING WAS IMMEDIATE

All of the healings in Acts were instantaneous; no recupera-

tive period was required. The afflicted were immediately restored to full health.

| Acts 3:7-8 | Acts 14:8-10 | Acts 20:9-12 |

UNBELIEVERS WERE HEALED

Acts 5:16   Acts 19:11-12
Acts 8:6-7   Acts 28:8-9

FAITH OF THE AFFLICTED HONORED

At times the faith of the afflicted was commended.

Acts 3:16   Acts 14:8-10

FAITH NOT NECESSARY

A personal faith was not necessarily required of the afflicted.

Acts 5:16   Acts 20:9-12
Acts 9:36-43   Acts 28:8-9
Acts 19:11-12

HEALINGS WERE UNDENIABLE

The miracles of healing were undeniable—even to the Sanhedrin.

Acts 4:15-17

SIN-RELATED SICKNESS

Sometimes God afflicted because of personal sin.

Acts 5:1-11   Acts 12:23
Acts 9:8   Acts 13:4-12

LIFE RESTORED

There were two resurrections.

Acts 9:36-43—Dorcas (by Peter)
Acts 20:9-12—Eutychus (by Paul)

SAINTS WERE ILL

Acts 9:36-43—Dorcas

HEALING IN ABSENTIA

Acts 19:11-12

The healing ministry in Acts is seemingly smaller than that of Christ, although it covered thirty years. On a comparative basis, Acts had more healings than the Old Testament—which ranged from creation to B.C. 400.

Appendix 4

The Epistles Healing Record

PURPOSE OF HEALING

Signs, miracles, and wonders were used to authenticate the apostles and their ministry (Romans 15:18-19; 2 Corinthians 12:12; Hebrews 2:4).

Spectacular supernatural healings were among the signs displayed by the apostles and those to whom they personally ministered. Whether the apostles themselves or those they ministered to did the signs, the signs were to attest the authority of the apostles as revealers of truth (see Acts 2:42-43).

If all Christians are supposed to perform such deeds, those deeds could not have served as the signs of apostleship (see 2 Corinthians 12:12). The signs attested their words as of equal authority with those of Jesus Himself, for He had chosen them as His spokesmen (see Matthew 10:11-15, 20, 40; 1 Corinthians 14:37).

HEALING DECLINED

Paul's frequency of healing declined with the passing of time.

Galatians 4:13-15—Paul was ill.
2 Corinthians 12:7-10—Paul was afflicted.
Philippians 2:25-30—Epaphroditus was ill.
1 Timothy 5:23—Timothy was ill.
2 Timothy 4:20—Trophimus was ill.

Healing is noticeable in the Old Testament, overwhelming in the gospels, frequent in Acts, and negligible in the epistles.

The apostolic age ended, and miraculous healing by direct human intervention ceased.

MEDICINE APPROVED

Paul recognized and recommended medicine.
1 Timothy 5:23

SIN-RELATED SICKNESS

James 5:14-20 outlines the biblical response to severe or untimely physical infirmities that might, but not necessarily, have their source in God's chastisement for personal sin.

Helpful Reading

Chantry, Walter J. *Signs of the Apostles: Observations on Pentecostalism Old and New*, 2d ed. Edinburgh: Banner of Truth, 1976.

Eareckson, Joni, and Estes, Steve. *A Step Further*. Grand Rapids: Zondervan, 1978.

Frost, Henry. *Miraculous Healing*. Reprint. London: Evangelical Press, 1972.

MacArthur, John F., Jr. *The Charismatics*. Grand Rapids: Zondervan, 1978.

Mayhue, Richard L. *The Biblical Pattern for Divine Healing*. Winona Lake, Ind.: BMH Books, 1979.

Murray, Andrew. *Divine Healing*. Reprint. Fort Washington, Pa.: Christian Literature Crusade, 1971.

Nolan, William A. *Healing: A Doctor in Search of a Miracle*. Greenwich, Conn.: Fawcett, 1976.

Short, A. Rendle. *The Bible and Modern Medicine*. Chicago: Moody, 1967.

Torrey, R. A. *Divine Healing*. Reprint. Grand Rapids: Baker, n.d.

Warfield, Benjamin B. *Counterfeit Miracles*. Reprint. London: Banner of Truth, 1972.

Scripture Index

Page numbers in boldface are found in Appendixes 1-4.

Moody Press, a ministry of the Moody Bible Institute, is designed for education, evangelization, and edification. If we may assist you in knowing more about Christ and the Christian life, please write us without obligation: Moody Press, c/o MLM, Chicago, Illinois 60610.